AF545001

GREAT BASEBALL STORIES

Today and Yesterday

Baseball has had a long and glorious history—a history filled with great players and spectacular achievements. Today's game also has superstars who have been challenging these past records. Read about the famous catchers of today and yesteryear—Thurman Munson and Johnny Bench, Mickey Cochrane and Yogi Berra; the powerful home run hitters Babe Ruth and Hank Aaron; the amazing base thieves like Maury Wills, Ty Cobb, and Lou Brock; and the incredible strikeout pitchers—Walter Johnson, Sandy Koufax, and Nolan Ryan. All this plus a look at the immortal Jackie Robinson and three superteams of the past and present—the 1927 Yankees, the 1934 Cardinals, and the 1976 Reds.

BOOKS BY BILL GUTMAN

Football Superstars of the '70s

Great Baseball Stories
Today and Yesterday

"My Father, the Coach" and Other Sports Stories

New Breed Heroes in Pro Baseball
New Breed Heroes of Pro Football

GREAT BASEBALL STORIES

Today and Yesterday

BILL GUTMAN

PHOTOGRAPHS

JULIAN MESSNER
NEW YORK

Published by Julian Messner
A Simon & Schuster Division of
Gulf & Western Corporation
Simon & Schuster Building
1230 Avenue of the Americas
New York, New York 10020

Designed by Irving Perkins

Manufactured in the United States of America
Second Printing, 1979

Library of Congress Cataloging in Publication Data

Gutman, Bill.
Great baseball stories.

1. Baseball stories. 2. Baseball players—
United States—Biography. I. Title.
GV873.G87 796.357'092'2 [B] 78-480
ISBN 0-671-32881-6

Contents

Introduction 7

CHAPTER 1 *Superstars in the Tools of Ignorance* 9

CHAPTER 2 *The .400 Club* 44

CHAPTER 3 *Thieves* 67

CHAPTER 4 *In Pursuit of the Babe and Other Home Run Sluggers* 89

CHAPTER 5 *The Flamethrowers—Baseball's Strikeout Kings* 116

CHAPTER 6 *Murderers' Row, the Gas House Gang, the Big Red Machine—A Trio of Superteams* 141

CHAPTER 7 *The One and Only Jackie* 169

Index 189

Introduction

Baseball, more than any other sport, has a long and honored tradition which goes back to the turn of the century. The legends of the game, whether they starred in 1910, 1940, or 1970, are still well-known to baseball fans everywhere. In fact, one of the favorite arguments among these diamond buffs is to compare players of the past with players of the present.

In one sense, it's an argument that can never be won or lost, because the game has changed, the stadiums have changed, the equipment has changed, and playing conditions have changed. But it's still a joy to ask questions such as could Cobb have hit Koufax, would Ruth hit sixty home runs today, could Walter Johnson strike out Rod Carew?

This book does not attempt to answer the questions. But it does look at various aspects of baseball down through the years and at some of the achievements of the older players that are being challenged or surpassed by players of today. And in that way perhaps readers will understand a bit more about the history of baseball and about the many great players who have graced the game down through the years.

For example, there has been only a handful of really great catchers in the game. Who were they and why were they great? How about fastball pitchers, flamethrowers? Here it's Walter Johnson, Sandy Koufax, and Nolan Ryan taking center stage. Then there're the home run hitters, notably Henry and the Babe, and also the base thieves, Cobb, Wills, and Lou Brock.

Will there ever be another .400 hitter? Ted Williams last did it in 1941. Can Rod Carew do it now? And what about the great teams of the game? Three of them are here—the 1927 Yankees, the 1934 Cardinals, and the 1976 Cincinnati Reds.

Finally, there's a separate chapter on a single man, a man whose courage and tenacity helped him overcome great odds and revolutionize not only baseball, but the entire sports world. His name is Jackie Robinson.

Great Baseball Stories: Today and Yesterday talks about all these things, and in doing so, looks at that long and glorious tradition and the many great players who have helped make baseball the national pastime.

CHAPTER 1

Superstars in the Tools of Ignorance

In the entire long history of baseball, the position that has the fewest superstars has to be catcher. That shouldn't be surprising. After all, what young man with any kind of smarts would want to catch? Not when there were so many glamour positions, like pitching, shortstop, or centerfield. By contrast, catching was brutal. The catcher had to squat down hundreds of times during a game, tens of thousands of times during a season. That took a big toll on the legs.

Then there was the equipment: a large glove, cumbersome shin guards, a suffocating chest protector, and a confining mask. Try wearing all that when the temperature and humidity reach ninety in August. All those pieces of equipment even had a nickname; they were called the "tools of ignorance." Why? Perhaps it meant that anyone dumb enough to catch deserved wearing the "tools."

But the apparatus wasn't even the whole story. Catchers were always in prime position to get hit with foul tips and wildly flung bats. Catchers were often bruised and battered

—hand and finger injuries were common. And when a runner came hurtling into home plate, it was the catcher's duty to get in the way, to block the plate. And so the immovable catcher took the brunt of the collision when the runner came in, spikes often aimed high. No, sir, catching was definitely not for the meek.

But it isn't all on the negative side. A good catcher is a *must* for any winning team, for he has tremendous responsibility. He has to be the team's field leader, the man who, more than any other, is aware of the entire game situation at all times. He must direct his fielders, remind them what to do on any given play, and alert them to possible arising situations. Then he must handle the pitchers, "call the game." He must know each and every hitter around the league, his strengths and weaknesses, and how each individual pitcher can best handle him. Then he must call for the best series of pitches. He has to judge what the pitcher has going for him that day.

The catcher must also have a strong, accurate throwing arm. He's got to be able to keep runners from stealing him blind. He must also be able to sense when a pitcher is tiring and be ready to offer his manager advice on making a change. So not only is it difficult to be a catcher, it also takes an extra special player to become a superstar at that position. Maybe that's why there have been so few of them down through the years.

In the very early days of the game, there were surely some good catchers. But it's hard to say now whether or not they were superstars. None of the early big names of the game—Cobb, Wagner, Speaker, Lajoie, Johnson, Mathewson, Young, Collins—were catchers. Old timers bring up names like Roger Bresnahan, Ray Schalk, or Gabby Street. But few fans today can recall anything outstanding that they may have done.

Then from the 1920s to the 1940s there were three men who clearly dominated the backstopping position. They were Gabby Hartnett, Mickey Cochrane, and Bill Dickey. These three were the first truly acknowledged superstar catchers. All three are now in the Hall of Fame, and many baseball people will pick from this trio when attempting to name the best ever.

In the late 1940s and into the '50s came two more outstanding catchers. Yogi Berra and Roy Campanella will never be forgotten. Their names are almost always linked—Berra and Campanella. They played for crosstown rivals, the New York Yankees and the Brooklyn Dodgers, and often found themselves behind the bat on opposite sides in the World Series.

Both Yogi and Campy won their league's Most Valuable Player award three times. Both now occupy a permanent niche at Cooperstown in baseball's Hall of Fame. Yet in a strange kind of way, these two set a pattern during their careers and for a few years afterward for the catchers who followed.

Berra and Campanella were built like fireplugs, short and stocky. Neither was particularly fast afoot. To many, they looked like they belonged behind the plate. More short and stocky catchers began appearing in the Bigs. In sandlot games or even little leagues, coaches would often pick the slow, heavy kids and make them the catchers.

While Berra and Campy dominated the catcher's spot, others were far behind. Those two could do it all—catch, hit, throw. But other less fortunate managers made do with catchers who could catch, if they were lucky, and do little else. It wasn't until the late 1960s that the position of catcher underwent a new, dramatic change. It did so in the person of one man. His name: Johnny Bench.

Bench came to the Cincinnati Reds as a nineteen-year-old in 1967. He became the first-string catcher a year later and has held that distinction since. Bench quickly brought to the position something it had lacked for years. He was a glamour player in an unglamorous position. Tall, handsome, and articulate, with a maturity far beyond his years, Bench proved himself a superstar within three seasons and became an idol to millions of youngsters. They wanted to play there. They wanted to be like Johnny Bench.

Others have followed Bench to the majors, catchers like Carlton Fisk of the Red Sox and Ted Simmons of the Cardinals. They, too, have helped dismiss some of the old myths about catchers and catching. Yet the other big catching superstar in today's game is something of a throwback to days gone by. He is Thurman Munson of the New York Yankees.

In a sense, Munson is built something like Yogi. In fact, he possesses many of the same skills as his predecessor. Thurman is a scrapper whose uniform is usually covered with dirt by game's end. But he, too, can do it all. As the leader of one of baseball's best teams, Munson reached a peak of his career in 1976 by leading the Yanks into the World Series and taking the American League's Most Valuable Player prize.

This has been—in a nutshell—a history of big league catching. Of course, there have been and are other fine catchers. But since these seven men do stand out on the lists of most experts, let's take a closer look at them and perhaps come to a better understanding of the difficult and usually unglamorous position of catcher.

Charles Leo "Gabby" Hartnett was born on December 20, 1900, in Woonsocket, Rhode Island. He grew up in Millville, Massachusetts, where his father was a streetcar conductor and later a bus driver. Gabby was the first of fourteen children. He was always a winner. As a teenager, he once won the amazing total of 55,000 marbles, playing against his friends.

He was also playing baseball by then. But he didn't think about the big leagues. He played semipro ball and went to work at the American Steel and Wire Mill in Worcester, Massachusetts. One morning in 1921, Gabby went off to work. The temperature was twenty degrees below zero. When he got to the mill, both his ears were frozen and he was in terrible pain.

"Right then and there I said no more work," recalled Gabby. "The whole thing made me angry."

In those days, baseball wasn't work, at least not for the men who played it. They loved the game, and although the money wasn't nearly what it is today, the pay then wasn't bad. So Gabby concentrated on catching for the Worcester team in the Eastern League that summer. Pretty soon the word went out that the 6-1, 218-pound youngster was a tough backstop. That's when the great John McGraw, manager of the New York Giants, sent a scout up to look at Gabby. The report that came in turned McGraw off. It read: "Hartnett won't make it. His hands are too small."

That didn't discourage the Chicago Cubs. They saw Hartnett as a potentially fine catcher and team leader. At the end of the 1921 season they signed him, buying his contract from Worcester for $2,500. The next season Gabby was in the Bigs.

Gabby was a colorful, flamboyant character, a center of

Gabby Hartnett (*Baseball Hall of Fame*)

attention wherever he went. When he was behind the plate you always knew he was there. Despite the constant squatting and bending, Gabby always stood erect, held his head high, and puffed his large chest way out. He often wore a smile on his face and displayed a confidence just short of cockiness.

Behind the plate he liked to talk to everyone in sight, and he loved to throw. The small hands didn't stop him from cutting down baserunners. He also loved to pepper the ball around the infield and would always fire it back to the mound. When a batter struck out, Gabby would raise the ball high with his right hand before starting it around the horn.

Hartnett was a good, though not great, hitter. His lifetime mark was .297, including six .300 seasons. His best was 1930 when he batted .339, belted 37 homers, and drove home 122 runs. That was a super season for him, the only one where he topped 30 homers and 100 RBIs.

It was his leadership and clutch play that really made Hartnett a Hall of Famer. For twelve seasons he caught 100 or more games for the Cubs. His zest for throwing hard almost cost him his career in 1929, when on the second day of spring training he let it all out and felt something snap in his arm. He missed virtually the entire year, but he came back better than ever in 1930.

Hartnett played in an era of greatness, playing with and against some of the diamond immortals. For instance, as a rookie in 1922, he caught the great Grover Cleveland Alexander, winner of 373 big league games.

"Alex was the best I caught at throwing with different speeds," Gabby said in later years. "He had about three speeds with the same pitch and it kept the hitters off balance."

Then there was the 1932 World Series, when Hartnett and his Cubs met the powerful New York Yankees. That was the Series in which Babe Ruth was said to have called his shot, pointing to a spot in the centerfield bleachers moments before hitting the ball there. The Cub pitcher that day was Charley Root; the catcher, Gabby Hartnett.

"The Babe didn't call his shot," Gabby always maintained. "It won't take anything away from the Babe because he helped all of us get good salaries. But I remember that Series. There was a lot of bench riding from both teams. And our guys were on the Babe pretty good when he came up.

"Babe got two strikes on him and our bench was really on his back. He looked at our dugout, not at centerfield, and he held up the index finger of his left hand, though pointing to the outfield. What he said was, 'It only takes one to hit.' Then, of course, he hit it."

The Yanks won that Series, but Gabby got some revenge in the 1934 All-Star Game. He was catching and the Giants lefty, Carl Hubbell, was facing the tough American League lineup. The first two batters got on base. Gabby called time and went to the mound.

"I told Hubbell, 'Why don't you throw the thing? It always gets me out.' "

The "thing" was Hubbell's famed screwball. King Carl started using it. He then struck out, in order, Ruth, Lou Gehrig, Jimmy Foxx, Al Simmons, and Joe Cronin. It was another piece of baseball history, and Gabby Hartnett was there, right behind the plate.

Gabby really showed his mettle during the 1938 season. In July of that year Charley Grimm stepped down as Cubs manager and suggested that Hartnett replace him. Gabby was named playing manager. The team was in third place

Mickey Cochrane (*Baseball Hall of Fame*)

that started the A's on a winning rally. They didn't win the pennant that year, but they were close, and Mickey Cochrane won the league's MVP prize when it was all over. In addition, he helped light a permanent fire under his teammates, for they went on to win three straight pennants after that and a couple of World Series.

It wasn't a quick trip to the Bigs for Mickey. He decided

to attend college first, an unusual thing for a ball player in those days. He went to Boston University, where he starred in baseball, football, basketball, track, and boxing. He did all this while working to pay for his schooling. After that he joined the Eastern Shore League where he used the name of Frank King. The year was 1923. Asked why he used another name, Mickey answered,

"If I was a flop nobody would know who I was, and I could start all over again someplace else."

That's how badly Mickey wanted to win. He wasn't even a catcher when he joined Dover. He played the infield. But when the team needed a catcher, Mickey volunteered. He would do anything to play and he made the most of it, hitting .322, while learning to catch at the same time.

The next year, 1924, Mickey batted .333 at Portland in the Pacific Coast League, and a year later he was in the majors. He hit right away, batting .331 as a rookie. But catching was another thing. You don't learn it overnight. Veteran catcher Cy Perkins worked a lot with Mickey that first year and talked about him.

"It was no wonder that Mike didn't know how to catch," said Perkins. "He hadn't been at it very long and didn't really know how to stand or shift. He was also too high behind the plate. I guess that made it easier for him to throw, but it's not a good enough target for pitchers who want to keep the ball low.

"It's not easy throwing from there when the ball is low, especially if the catcher's knee is down. But Mike worked at throwing them out from down low until he was blue in that tomato face instead of red. And he became great at it."

No one ever questioned Mickey's ability to lead. In the

pennant seasons of 1929–1931, he batted .331, .357 and .349. Years later, manager Connie Mack said of Mickey:

"More than any other player, he was responsible for the three pennants we won in those years."

Yet when things went wrong, Mickey brooded. He took the A's 1931 Series loss to the Cardinals very hard. The fact that the Redbirds' Pepper Martin had stolen five bases stuck in Cochrane's craw, even though everyone knew Martin ran on the A's pitchers, not on Mickey.

Mickey's career took a change in 1934. Connie Mack was breaking up his great Philadelphia team and Mickey was sold to Detroit. But he not only went as a player. The Tigers wanted him as their manager as well as a player. It was Mickey's childhood dream come true.

Not only did Mickey hit .320 his first year at Detroit, he also managed the team to the American League pennant. Unfortunately, the Cards whipped the Tigers in the World Series. Mickey raged once more.

The next year, however, was something else. With Mickey batting .319, the Tigers won the pennant, then the World Series from the Chicago Cubs. Mickey had been in the majors for eleven years, and had been on five pennant winners. This was to be the beginning of the end of his great days, however.

In 1936 the fires that raged within Mickey caught up with him. He suffered a nervous breakdown and played in just forty-four games. He was trying to make a comeback in 1937 at the age of thirty-four and was batting .306 in late May. The Tigers were playing the Yanks and Mickey homered off New York's Bump Hadley. The next time up he crowded the plate, from the left side as usual, hoping to pull the ball behind the runner on first.

Hadley threw a fastball that sailed up and in. Mickey lost it and it crashed into his temple, an inch or so above his right eye. He fell to the ground. He woke up in the clubhouse and asked to return to the game. Then he passed out once more and didn't wake up for ten days.

Mickey's skull was fractured in three places. He was lucky to be alive, and his doctor advised he never play ball again. He didn't.

Mickey returned to manage the Tigers again, but he wasn't happy, since he couldn't get out on the field and show the players what he wanted. The Tigers released him as manager in August 1938. He returned to baseball briefly now and then, but it was never the same. For Mickey Cochrane, with his .320 lifetime average and all those marvelous skills behind the plate, belonged on a ballfield. He died at age fifty-nine in 1962.

The man closest to the play that fateful day in 1937 when Mickey Cochrane was beaned was the Yankee catcher, Bill Dickey. Dickey was the first to reach his fallen rival, and to many that scene showed one of the two greatest American League catchers looking down on the other.

Dickey played seventeen seasons for the New York Yankees and lost two more to military service in World War II. During his career he had a lifetime batting average of .313, batted over .300 on eleven occasions, and knocked in more than 100 runs for four straight seasons.

Dickey could also catch. Besides having all the skills, Dickey had the memory for the game that all the great backstops seem to possess. For instance, after the Yanks had won the 1943 World Series from the Cardinals, Bill stepped into

Bill Dickey (*New York Yankees*)

an elevator at the Chase Hotel in St. Louis. A soldier got on the elevator, looked at Dickey, and said:

"I'll bet you don't remember me."

The soldier was a former major leaguer who did not last very long, an easy man to forget. But Dickey took one look at the man and said, "I can't remember your name, but I know how we pitched to you."

Unlike many catchers, Dickey was tall and slim, standing nearly 6-2 and weighing just 185 pounds. He kidded skeptics by saying that no one would be able to throw one over his head.

Dickey was also extremely quick behind the plate. He could make a fast move, yet retain his balance for a throw or subsequent movement. He had a quick arm which developed into an accurate one, and he was one of the first catchers to get rid of the traditional large, heavy catcher's mitt for a light, smaller one, which he could maneuver much better.

As the years went on, Dickey learned many more tricks of his trade. Most catchers give the target to the pitcher with their glove. But it's easy to develop the habit of holding the target higher for a fastball and lower for a curve. A shrewd hitter can sometimes spot this with a quick glance. Dickey crossed them up.

"I told our pitchers to throw at my knee on a curve so that I could cross up the batter by keeping my hands high."

Bill had a good start as a catcher, for his father was a pitcher and catcher in the minor leagues and helped Bill. The younger Dickey was born on June 6, 1907, at Bastrop, Louisiana, but he grew up in Kensett, Arkansas.

Bill played the game early, but when he was in high school he was a pitcher and second baseman. It was at Little Rock College that Bill and a friend, Jimmy Foley, began taking turns pitching and catching with one another. One day Bill took his friend's place behind the plate with the Hot Springs team, and a scout saw him make a powerful, but wild throw. He liked the way the tall youngster handled himself and signed the eighteen-year-old Dickey to a contract with Little Rock of the Southern Association. The year was 1925. Three years later Dickey was with the Yankees.

Bill's Yankee career spanned two eras. He came up when the Bronx Bombers had their famed Murderers' Row lineup, featuring Ruth, Gehrig, Meusel, Combs, and the rest. He closed his career in the 1940s when the New Yorkers had the likes of DiMaggio, Rolfe, Rizzuto, Gordon, Keller. Dickey contributed mightily to both Yankee outfits.

As a young player he once barely beat the boastful Ruth in a footrace, and another time he almost tangled with the Babe when he broke a raw egg in one of the Bambino's shoes. Those kinds of pranks were a big part of baseball in the earlier days.

Bill's best years were the middle to late '30s, 1936–1939, when the Yanks were putting together a string of four straight World Series triumphs. The tall catcher batted .362 in '36 and the next year hit .332 with 29 homers and 133 RBIs.

In 1943, Dickey was still good enough to hit .351 in 85 games, but like so many other big leaguers of the day, he then entered military service. When he returned for the 1946 season, he was nearly thirty-nine years old. It was just about over. He managed the team briefly that year, then retired. He returned three years later and served as a coach for eight seasons, witnessing the growth of still another Yankee dynasty.

Bill didn't have to worry about Yankee catching the year

he retired. It would soon be once again in very able hands. The Bombers had a young rookie that year, a strange-looking little man named Yogi Berra.

Dickey, in fact, remembers young Yogi well. "When Yogi first broke in," said Dickey, "he used to throw high to second base. The ball would often sail into the outfield. The reason was that he was stepping back before making the throw. He wasn't properly balanced. Once he learned to move in, the ball went down and to the bag. That's when Yogi became one of the better throwers in the league."

Yogi was good at a lot of things. As a catcher, he handled the tough Yank pitching staff without a flaw. As a hitter, he was especially dangerous in clutch situations. In fact, during the Yankee heyday in the '50s, many pitchers said they feared Berra more than the awesome Mickey Mantle when the game was on the line.

Larry "Yogi" Berra was an unlikely superstar. Short and squat, he had a good-natured round face with large ears. He almost looked like a comic book character. He had his own way of speaking and would often make good-natured slips that made him seem not too bright, which was certainly not the case. One of the classics came early in his career when some of his friends and family from his native St. Louis honored him before the Yanks took on the old Browns. A humble Berra took the microphone and said:

"I want to thank all the baseball fans and everyone else who made this night necessary."

Sometimes Yogi made light of his exploits on the diamond. The Yanks were playing the Browns one night and the St. Louis club had a runner on third. The batter tried a squeeze bunt. Yogi pounced on the ball and lunged at the batter, tagging him out, then he dove back at the plate and tagged the sliding runner. It was a brilliant, unassisted double play. When asked how he did it, Yogi said:

"I just tagged everything in sight, including the umpire."

Don't think for a minute that Yogi wasn't acutely aware of everything that was happening in a game, day in and day out. There wasn't much he'd forget when it came to batters and pitchers. Late in his career Yogi bruised a thumb and they took him to the hospital for x-rays. As Yogi and the Yankee doctor were walking down the corridor, they met a Dr. Ames, who had once pitched in the Yankee organization. The Yankee doctor said hello to Dr. Ames, and suddenly Yogi piped up:

"I remember you," he said. "I hit a home run off you on a change-up."

Yogi was referring to an incident some twelve years earlier when he was playing service ball. That's the memory of a catcher for you.

Lawrence Peter Berra was born on May 12, 1925, in a section of St. Louis known as The Hill. His best friend during his growing-up years was Joe Garagiola, who also made the majors, but later made more of a name for himself as an announcer and television personality. The two boys spent most of their time together, playing ball and running around the streets. As Garagiola recalled, Yogi was a fine athlete even then.

"Yog could kick the ball the farthest in football, the hardest in soccer, and was the best hitter in baseball. I remember us playing football once against some kids with full equipment. We had nothing, not even helmets. Well, Yogi butted heads with a kid who had everything, and this kid started crying, took off his helmet, and went home."

Yogi settled on baseball. He played with Norfolk of the

Yogi Berra (*New York Yankees*)

Piedmont League in 1943, spent two years in the service, and then signed with the Yankees. He came up briefly at the end of the 1946 season, and the next year was there to stay. At 5-8, 190 pounds, the squat Berra was the butt of many practical jokes and jibes his first year or so. But he laughed most of them off and was soon a respected member of baseball's most powerful team.

When Yogi was at his peak from about 1950 to 1958, he caught an amazing number of games without rest, yet continued to hit well. In that period he won the American League MVP prize three times.

He was especially tough in the World Series, and no one liked to see old number 8 standing on the left side of the plate when the chips were down. In the 1956 World Series against the Dodgers, Yogi not only caught Don Larsen's perfect game, but managed to hit .360 with three homers and 10 RBIs.

A notorious bad ball hitter, Yogi slammed two circuits in the '56 Series against Don Newcombe in the seventh game. The second shot came on a pitch low and away that left both Newcombe and Roy Campanella shaking their heads. As he circled the bases, Yogi knew the kind of pitch he hit. He looked over at the dejected Newcombe and shouted:

"It wasn't your fault, Newk. It wasn't your fault!"

Yogi managed to hit .293 in 1963, his final season as a player, and he left with a .285 lifetime mark and 358 home runs, among his other accomplishments. He managed the Yanks in 1964, taking them to a pennant. After a World Series loss, however, he was dismissed. He became a coach and later manager of the expansionist New York Mets, and in 1976 he returned to his beloved Yankees once again as a coach. Back at the Stadium in the Bronx, Yogi is always greeted by a wealth of cheers. The fans remember him and all those magic moments when he was one of the best catchers in baseball.

If Berra had a rival for catching supremacy during the 1950s that rival had to be Roy Campanella. Campy was a smiling, happy, energetic black man who belted the ball for the mighty Brooklyn Dodgers in their glory years. Like the Yog, Campy was a compact, powerful man, standing just 5-9½, but weighing in the neighborhood of 205 pounds and up.

He was a few years older than Yogi, having been born on November 19, 1921, in Philadelphia. Roy came to the majors two years later than Yogi. The reason was simple. Before 1947, there were no black players in the major leagues. Campy came up in 1948, a year after Jackie Robinson had broken baseball's so-called color line.

Campy only played for ten seasons. He might have gone on for a few more years, for in 1958 the Dodgers moved to Los Angeles where the climate was wonderful and the left field wall very close to home plate. They say Campy would have flourished there. But destiny had another idea.

Shortly before leaving for spring training, Campy was driving home from his Harlem liquor store. His car skidded on a curve and wrapped itself around a telephone pole. The badly injured Campanella was taken to a hospital where it was discovered he had broken his neck. Campy would not only never play baseball again, he would never walk again.

It was a bitter blow for Roy, whose early life hadn't been especially easy. He left home at age fifteen to play with the Bacharach Giants, a Philadelphia Negro team. It was to be just a short barnstorming trip, but while in New York, the manager of the Baltimore Elite Giants of the Negro National League asked Campy to try out. Roy was signed. He was paid just $60 a month to play with the Giants. But he couldn't complain, since in those days a young black man had no hopes of playing in the major leagues.

Life in the Negro Leagues wasn't easy. The players traveled the country in buses, always uncertain about where they'd eat, where they'd sleep, and where they'd be allowed to freshen up. Campy was already a catcher, of course, and learned to play with an abundance of painful injuries. "You only got paid when you played," he said.

In the winters he went down to the Caribbean and played there, earning some $45 a week, better money than he made at home. It looked like that was the way it would always be—until 1945. That's when Campy played for a Negro team against some major leaguers, and Branch Rickey, boss of the Dodgers, asked to see him.

Rickey already had his plan to break the color line and had all but picked Robinson to be the one. But he knew in his heart it would work and wanted more good black players behind Jackie. He signed Campy and big Don Newcombe for starters. In 1946, Roy was at Nashua of the New England League. Rickey cautioned Roy and Newk about possible racial problems, but things as a whole worked well in New England. A rival catcher once threw some dirt in Roy's face, but the usually affable Campy settled that fast.

"Try that again," he snarled at the man, "and I'll beat you to a pulp."

The only thing Campy did beat to a pulp was the baseball, hitting .290 with 13 homers and 96 RBIs in 113 games. He was the league's Most Valuable Player, and two years later was doing his catching in Brooklyn. The Dodgers had a powerful team in those days, though they always seemed frustrated by the Yankees in the World Series, losing to the Bombers in 1947, 1949, 1952, and 1953. They finally cracked through and won one in 1955. The players on that team are legends. Besides Campy there were Robinson, Duke Snider, Pee Wee Reese, Gil Hodges, Carl Furillo, Billy Cox, Don

Roy Campanella (*Baseball Hall of Fame*)

Newcombe, Preacher Roe, Joe Black, Clem Labine, Jim Gilliam, and others.

As a catcher, Campy was tops. He praised his pitchers and gave them confidence. He was tough on low pitches and could block the plate like a Mack truck. And he could throw. In the 1949 World Series he picked off the Yanks best baserunner, Phil Rizzuto. Said the Scooter:

"That's the first time in my life I've ever been picked off third base. What an arm that Campanella has!"

Campy also had some banner seasons behind the plate. In 1951 he won his first MVP award with a .325 average, 33 homers, and 108 RBIs. Two years later he was at it again with a .312 mark, 41 homers, and 142 RBIs. Two years after that his numbers read .318, 32, and 107. He was MVP each time.

There were also some off years when Campy played with bad injuries, but during his all-too-brief career he belted 242 homers and had a lifetime mark of .276. By comparison, Yogi Berra hit 358 lifetime homers, but never went over 30 in a single season. Campy was over that four times. If he had started sooner and finished later, there's no telling what he might have done.

Roy remained in the public eye despite his accident. The Dodgers were good to him, giving him a night out in Los Angeles that saw some 93,000 fans come into the old Coliseum, the proceeds helping to pay Campy's medical bills. Since then, and despite his confinement to a wheelchair, Roy has remained active. He's been on television and has worked to help youngsters stay in school and find jobs. He's also put in appearances at the Dodgers' spring training camp to help look over the catching prospects. For that job, you couldn't find a better man than Roy Campanella.

The next supercatchers are the two men playing in today's game: Johnny Bench and Thurman Munson. Both are certainly well known to today's fans, but let's take a brief look anyway.

Johnny Bench was born on December 7, 1947, in the tiny town of Binger, Oklahoma. He grew up there, a place where there was really nothing else to do but play sports. Baseball was always his favorite. In fact, all John ever wanted to be was a major league ball player.

It was his father, Ted Bench, who first turned him on to catching. Mr. Bench knew that there would always be a need for good catchers in the Bigs. There were those who could catch, but not hit; and those who could hit, but not catch. The right balance was always hard to find. Mr. Bench had also been a semipro catcher himself, so he could coach his son on the finer points of the position.

He worked very hard on young John's throwing. He taught his son how to grip the ball across the seams to get maximum speed on his throws. He also had him practice throwing to spots and from a catcher's crouch, not standing up. It got so John could throw up to 250 feet from a crouch.

Shortly after Johnny graduated from Binger High School in 1965, the Cincinnati Reds signed him to a contract, giving him a $10,000 bonus. But as a good friend of his said, "He would have gone just for the price of a plane ticket."

John flew to Tampa to a Class A team at the age of seventeen. He got there while a game was in progress, dressed, and caught the ninth inning of the game. He learned right then and there that he had to grow up real fast.

"I was out on the same ballfield with a lot of guys twenty-four and twenty-five years old. Many of them knew they weren't going anywhere in baseball. It was already too late

Johnny Bench (*Cincinnati Reds*)

for them. They had a lot of gripes and I had to be careful.

"I was in a man's game, no place for a boy of seventeen. I was doing a man's job and getting a man's salary. So I had to act the part or get burned. Ever since that first game I've been a regular catcher doing a man's job."

John did well that first year. In fact, Yogi Berra saw him play a few times and remarked, "He can do it all right now."

A handsome, solid 6-footer, weighing some 190 pounds, John looked like a movie star as much as an athlete. He stood deep in the batter's box on the right side and took a big cut at the ball. He had power. Defensively, he was already outstanding, quick as a cat, with a fast glove and rifle arm. He became Minor League Player of the Year in 1967, came up to the Reds at the tail end of the season, and claimed the regular catcher's job the next year. At the age of twenty, he was ready.

Johnny knew a big league catcher had to be a take-charge guy. He showed that his first year. He soon let his pitchers know he was the boss. When veteran Jim Maloney was on the mound with two strikes on a hitter, Bench called for a curve.

"I figure I can throw another fastball right by him," recalled Maloney, "so I shook John off. But he signaled for the curve again. I shook him off. He signaled for it once more, so I threw it and the batter fans the breeze. Back in the dugout he just sort of smiled at me.

"Well, here was this kid, still wet behind the ears, and he's actually bawling me out and telling me what to do. He did it all year long. He was like another coach to me. And you know something, I liked it."

There was all kinds of praise for John that first year, most of it for his poise, his throwing arm, and his general catching ability. But he was also good enough to hit .275 with 15 homers and 82 RBIs. He was the National League's Rookie of the Year and also won the Golden Glove award as the league's best catcher.

John always paid special attention to his catching. He studied it and made it an art. For instance, although he's not a small man, he gets down lower than any catcher in baseball. That allows him to keep his glove lower and gives his pitcher a better target. He is constantly smoothing spike marks in front of the plate so low pitches will not take bad hops.

He also rarely catches warm-ups, and if he does he makes sure he's wearing all his gear.

"Some catchers warm up the pitcher without their equipment," he explains. "So when there's a pitch in the dirt they duck out of the way and swipe at it. That makes for bad habits. If you want to warm up a pitcher you better catch him just as you would in a real game."

John also began using the new, one-hand style of catching. For years the traditional way to grab a pitch was with both hands. But that led to many hand and finger injuries from foul tips and short hops. A Cubs catcher, Randy Hundley, was the first to start using one hand, but it was Johnny Bench who really refined it.

The style calls for a larger, hinged mitt, something like a first baseman's. This is used to snare everything. The bare hand is kept protected behind the glove or outside the right knee. John became an expert at this and at sweeping the ball from the mitt to his bare hand for a throw.

Johnny's other exploits are well known. He has twice won the National League's MVP award, with great seasons. In 1970 he hit .293 with 45 homers and 148 RBIs, and two years later batted .270 with 40 round trippers and 125 ribbys. He has become an integral part of Cincinnati's Big Red Machine, the best team in baseball during the early and mid-1970s, helping them to a pair of world championships. In fact, during the 1976 sweep of the New York Yankees, Bench was Series' MVP.

But even if he couldn't hit a lick, Johnny Bench would still be valuable. For rarely, if ever, does a catcher come along who can do so many things behind the plate so well.

One other catcher who also does many things well is Thurman Munson, the main man on the New York Yankees. Munson follows a great tradition, which started with Bill Dickey and moved on to Yogi Berra. To many, Munson is their equal.

Thurman is a scrapper, a fighter, a battler. He's a stocky 5-11, 190-pounder who often sulks because he feels he doesn't look as good as some of the so-called glamour boys of the game. But he does things as well, that's for sure.

Munson was born on June 7, 1947, in Akron, Ohio. His father was a truck driver who had to work hard for a living. Yet Thurman always credits his father for his success.

"My father was a go-getter," said Thurman. "I think he's the one who made me want to play hard. He always wanted me to do better. He wanted me to improve and he'd always tell me what I was doing wrong."

Surprisingly, and unlike Johnny Bench, Thurman wasn't a catcher until his senior year in high school. He stayed away from the position for the usual reasons. He'd rather play shortstop and second base. But in his senior year the team needed a catcher very badly. Always a team man, Thurman volunteered to don the tools of ignorance.

Thurman Munson (*New York Yankees*)

He surprised everyone, including himself, at how quickly he took to the new position. He also found he enjoyed it back there, because he was in the game at all times and could really be a leader. Once he mastered the fundamentals, he improved rapidly.

Thurm went to Kent State University on a baseball scholarship and continued his catching. He was soon an outstanding player attracting major league scouts. One of the scouts was former Yankee, Gene Woodling. The year was 1968 and Woodling knew the Yanks needed a catcher. Yogi had retired in 1963, and his successor, Elston Howard, a fine, but aging catcher, had been traded to Boston. The spot was open.

Woodling was asked what he first saw in Munson at Kent State.

"The first thing I noticed about Thurman was his speed," said Woodling. "He was exceptionally fast for a catcher. Catchers can sometimes get away with being slow, but this kid could run.

"Then I noticed his arm. It was strong—not the strongest I'd ever seen, but strong enough. The thing about it was the quickness. Thurm had, and still has, the quickest arm I've ever seen on a catcher, and I think he's proved it in the big leagues. Anyway, when I saw him throw I was just about convinced."

Woodling watched Thurman some more. He saw that the youngster already had outstanding ability as a catcher. "Defensively, he was major league caliber."

A veteran player, who had been a teammate with Dickey and Berra, thought Thurman had major league catching ability, yet Munson had only been behind the plate for a couple of years. He came fast.

The Yanks signed Thurman in 1968 and sent him to their Binghamton farm club. In 71 games he batted .301 and caught very well. The next year he was at Syracuse, the Yanks' top farm club in the International League. He played 28 games there, hit .363, and was then called up to the big club. He had played only 99 minor league games and was ready. When asked about his rapid advancement, Thurm growled:

"You don't get rich playing in Syracuse."

But it was pride and desire more than money that drove Munson. He always felt he had to prove himself again and again. He was a backup catcher for the remainder of '69, but the next year he won the regular job. He was catching well, but hitting terribly. He got just one hit in his first thirty at bats. But the Yanks stuck with him. Maybe it was his cockiness. When a reporter asked about his one for thirty start, Munson said coolly:

"Don't worry about me. When the year is over I'll be hitting .300."

It was a brash prediction, but sure enough, soon afterward Munson began to hit, and he hit well. By season's end he had his average up to .302, including six homers and 53 RBIs. His catching was strong all year long. Many compared him with the National League's new star catcher, Johnny Bench.

"I remember reading stories about Bench chewing out his pitchers as a rookie," said one Yank hurler. "Well, this kid [Munson] is the same way. If he feels you're not putting out, or not doing something right, he lets you know about it in no uncertain terms. He's not afraid to speak out."

Thurman also followed Bench's lead and was named American League Rookie of the Year. The following season Thurm had some trouble at the bat, hitting just .251. But he showed that he was a catcher to be reckoned with behind the plate.

He led all receives in both leagues with a .998 fielding mark, committing just a single error in 615 chances. He also threw out 23 of the 38 runners who tried to steal on him.

The Yanks still weren't a pennant team, though. When Boston got a hot rookie catcher named Carlton Fisk in 1972, a lot of the spotlight faded from Munson. In fact, a feud formed between the two. After Fisk's hot rookie year, Thurm's stats were always better. But it seems that it took many fans a while to realize that. They kept voting the handsome Fisk to the all-star team while Thurman fumed.

But in 1973 Thurm hit .301, with 20 homers and 74 RBIs. Fisk hit just .246 with 26 homers and 71 ribbys. The edge went to Munson. Before the 1974 season, Yankee broadcaster and former player Bill White had this to say about Munson.

"Bench is the only catcher in either league who might be better than Munson right now. Anybody like Thurm, who uses the whole field to hit, is a good hitter. Look at the guys who always hit .300. They hit the ball all over. Munson does that, too."

Hand and elbow problems slowed Munson in '74, but in the next two years he really came into his own. In 1975 he batted .318 with 12 homers and 102 big RBIs. The next year, 1976, Munson led the Yanks to their first pennant since 1964. He did it with a .302 average, 17 homers, and 105 RBIs. For his efforts he was named the American League's Most Valuable Player. With Johnny Bench having a .234 off year, Thurm had to be the best catcher in the majors.

Ironically, Bench and the Reds stole Munson's thunder in the World Series. Cincy swept the Series in four games, with

Bench getting hot and winning the Series MVP prize. Munson, however, was the only Yankee hitting, getting nine Series hits in just four games, for a .529 average. He had given it his all. That's the only way he knows how to play the game.

That's the story of seven catching immortals who spanned nearly sixty years of major league baseball. Can you compare Munson and Bench with, say, Hartnett and Cochrane? That's a tough one. After all, the game has changed somewhat during those years, as well.

One thing is certain. There just aren't too many other great catchers running around. These men stand out, in their own time and now. Perhaps these brief glimpses of each have shown why catching is possibly the most difficult of all the positions to play well, day in and day out.

These seven men have been superstars at the backstopping position. It hasn't been easy for them. They've all been battered, bruised, and beaten at one time or another. But they've all come back to star again. Each in his own way has helped make himself and the game of baseball great.

CHAPTER 2

The .400 Club

There are all kinds of clubs in this world—country clubs, bridge clubs, boys' clubs, cheese clubs, golf clubs, book clubs, record clubs. You name it and there's a club for it somewhere.

There is one particular club where the membership has always been small and is getting smaller. In fact, some say there'll never be another new member in this club, although there are many men who'd love to join.

It's the .400 Club, open only to major league baseball players who have batted .400 or better over the course of a single season.

Most of the members joined in the early days of the game. There was even a period when the club was fairly active. After 1900, the members of the .400 Club could be counted on your fingers. Only eight men in the history of the game since 1900 have hit the magic mark. Their names read like a Hall of Fame Who's Who: Ty Cobb, Rogers Hornsby, Napoleon Lajoie, Joe Jackson, George Sisler, Harry Heilmann, Bill Terry, and Ted Williams. (Jackson is not in the Hall because he was involved in the Black Sox Scandal of 1919.)

These are modern baseball's .400 hitters. Cobb and Hornsby each did it three times, and not coincidentally, they have the two highest lifetime averages ever compiled, .367 for Cobb, and .358 for Hornsby. Sisler was a two-time .400 man, while the others did it once each.

Hornsby had the highest mark, a .424 season in 1924. Lajoie managed a .422 in 1901, while Cobb and Sisler each checked in with a .420 season. Jackson once hit .408 and didn't win the batting title, because Cobb hit .420 that year. Likewise, Cobb hit .401 in 1922 and finished second to Sisler's .420. In a sense, the years between 1911 and 1925 were the golden years for .400 hitters. Lajoie came before that, but only two came after. They were Bill Terry's .401 in 1930, the last National Leaguer to join the club; and Ted Williams' .406 in 1941, making the Splendid Splinter the last American and major leaguer to ever reach the magical mark.

Years have melted into more years since Ted Williams had his .400 season and the nagging question remains. Will anyone ever hit the mark again?

There have certainly been enough great ball players in the nearly forty years since Williams turned the trick. Just look at some of the names: DiMaggio, Musial, Robinson, Appling, Mays, Mantle, Aaron, Clemente, Yastrzemski, Rose, Oliva. All were batting champs, but none ever reached .400. In fact, the man who came closest was none other than the same Ted Williams, when he registered a .388 mark in 1957 at the age of thirty-nine.

In the mid-1970s the .400 question isn't asked as often. But when it is, the name comes up. It is the almost unanimous opinion of baseball people everywhere that the only player in today's game with an honest shot at a .400 season is Rod Carew of the Minnesota Twins.

Why Carew, and not Pete Rose, Cesar Cedeno, Bill Madlock, George Brett, or any of the other good average hitters of today? Perhaps it's because Carew's style of hitting is closest to being a throwback to the old days, to the style used by the Cobbs and Hornsbys, the men who did make it into the club.

Before talking about Carew and the reasons he has a shot to hit .400, let's turn back the clock and take a look at the game when men did reach the big mark. It was a substantially different kind of ball game.

For starters, most of the .400 action came in the era of the so-called dead ball. The baseball itself was made differently and didn't jump off the bats the same way it did in later years. It took a real clout to produce a home run, so there was not the same kind of emphasis on the circuit shot. With the home run eliminated as the ultimate, sudden, game-winning weapon, hitters had to resort to other things.

The result, as some people like to put it, was pure baseball. Every element of attack was used—the bunt, hit and run, sacrifice, opposite field hitting. Players became experts at manipulating the bat. They made adjustments in the batter's box, shifted their feet, and often changed their stances to accommodate game situations. They didn't just dig in and swing from the heels. Baseball was more of a thinking game then than it is today.

There were other differences, too. Hitters had more of an advantage in earlier days. For one thing, the fields were all grass and dirt; there were no artificial surfaces. The often rough and unkempt condition they were in made for more bad hops. Also, the gloves were smaller and didn't have those huge pockets that could trap everything.

The pitchers had advantages though, too. The balls

weren't thrown out of play as soon as they had a little mark or scuff on them. They'd often be retained until they were bruised and battered or fouled into the stands. A marked-up ball will definitely do more tricks than a new, clean one. In addition, there were no rules against spitballs, emery balls, and other such manipulations. Many of the pitchers doctored the ball to give it that extra hop, skip, and jump.

Yet it was no coincidence that men like Cobb and Hornsby compiled astronomical batting averages year after year. They studied hitting, making it an art, and never stopped practicing and looking for ways to improve until the day they quit. As Cobb himself once said of baseball:

"The Great American Game should be an unrelenting war of nerves."

The old-time players played for keeps. A guy like Ty Cobb was always looking for ways to get another hit, to outfox the pitchers and the fielders. Ty was a lefty swinger. He had a basic stance that he could change at a moment's notice, but that didn't affect his hitting.

Cobb's secret was balance. He always strove for it, no matter how he stood in there. Basically, he kept his feet fairly close together, maybe fourteen inches apart at the most. Yet he was always ready to shift them to a different position depending on the pitcher and game situation. He wanted to be highly mobile in the box, ready to open or close the stance or shift into position for a bunt.

When Ty wanted to hit to left field he'd drop his rear foot back and choke up more on the bat. He used an open grip, his hands several inches apart, so he could come up or down on the bat in an instant. If he wanted to pull the ball to right field he simply moved his front foot back and dropped his hand on the bat.

Ty Cobb (*Baseball Hall of Fame*)

Ty had all kinds of other tricks. For instance, he never used the same stance twice in a row. That way he figured he'd confuse the pitcher just enough so that the hurler wouldn't know exactly what Ty was planning to do. Cobb also believed in holding his arms away from his body. He said that gave him more bat mobility, made it easier for him to adjust his swing.

Another of Ty's favorite weapons was the bunt. He practiced his bunting continuously and then used it to his complete advantage.

First of all, he used it for base hits. Ty felt a bunt was the hardest play for a third baseman to handle. He could also use it as a decoy, to draw the third baseman in, allowing him to slash the ball past him. He also felt that the bunt could cool off a hot pitcher by making him lose his concentration; having to field a few bunts and throw to first might affect the pitcher's rhythm.

Lastly, Ty bunted when he was in one of his rare batting slumps. It enabled him to put bat on ball, regain his confidence, and even get a few base hits along the way.

Then there was the psychological Cobb. He used everything to get the best of a pitcher. For instance, Big Ed Walsh was a spitball pitcher in the early days who met with great success. Ty was having a terrible time hitting Walsh. He figured he had to know when the spitter was coming. Finally, he learned how to do it. The key was knowing when Walsh was faking the spitter or really planning to throw it.

"It was his cap," said Ty in later years. "When he faked the spitter it didn't move. But when he really loaded up he'd open his mouth and the bill of his cap would rise slightly. By watching carefully I could detect this and finally wound up with a .307 lifetime mark against Big Ed."

Against Walter Johnson, the great Washington fastballer, Ty really had to do some thinking. At first Ty was having no luck with Johnson at all. No one hit the Big Train very well. Finally, Ty found a weakness.

"There were times when I all but shut my eyes and swung against Walter," he admitted. "Then one day he accidentally beaned one of my teammates, Oscar Vitt. Oscar went down like a wet rag and didn't move. I watched Walter run to the plate and stand there as white as a sheet until Oscar woke up. The big guy was totally frightened of his own speed. He thought he might have killed Vitt and was so upset that he took himself out of the game.

"That got me to thinking. Walter was such a nice guy that he'd never consider brushing a hitter back, much less throw at his head. It was a weakness that I could exploit. So instead of standing my usual ten inches from the plate, I began moving in on Walter until I was practically standing on the dish. This cut down Walter's strike zone. I was gambling that he'd be afraid of hitting me and try to work the outside corner.

"That's what happened. And whenever he got behind on me, say two balls and no strikes, I'd move back to my normal position and wait for him to groove one. It worked. Never in a million years did I expect to dominate Walter Johnson. But soon I was hitting him better and I don't think he ever figured out why. But my lifetime average against him was around .325. Without my plate-crowding, I don't think it would have been higher than .125."

Ty used everything and used it well to get that unbelievable .367 lifetime average over 24 seasons, 12 batting titles, 4,191 base hits, and three .400-plus seasons.

Rogers Hornsby was a right-handed hitter who didn't use quite as much guile as Cobb. Yet he made hitting his own science and never stopped working to improve. Though Hornsby didn't play regularly as long as Ty and didn't get nearly as many hits, he was nevertheless a devastating batter. A line drive hitter with more power than Ty, the Rajah had the second-best lifetime mark, .358.

From 1921 to 1925, Hornsby was probably the greatest hitter who ever lived. In those five years he had batting marks of .397, .401, .384, .424, and .403. It all comes out to an average of .402 for a five-year period, an incredible batting feat never duplicated.

The Rajah wanted every edge he could get. He had keen eyesight and wouldn't do anything to jeopardize it. During his career he never went to a movie. The "flicks" actually flickered in those days and Rog thought the flickering lights could hurt his eyes. He also read very little for the same reason. Though he loved going to the races, he always had someone else read the small print on the racing form.

Legend has it that even the umpires respected Hornsby's eyes. One time a pitcher thought he had a third strike on Rajah. But since Hornsby didn't swing, the ump called a ball, figuring it had missed the mark. The pitcher, of course, complained about the call. Then on the next pitch Hornsby hit the ball out of the park. Said the umpire to the pitcher:

"You see, Mr. Hornsby will tell you when it's close enough to be called a strike."

Hornsby had an unusual batting stance. He stood way to the rear of the batter's box, in the back corner, and strode into the ball.

"Because of the stance," he said in later years, "they all

Rogers Hornsby (*Baseball Hall of Fame*)

thought I was a sucker for a pitch low and away. But I wasn't, not the way I stepped into the ball.

"Actually, the pitch I didn't like was high and tight, but by stepping into the ball, then pulling away from it when it was up and in, I often got a break from the umpires."

Hornsby was a vicious line drive hitter. The old timers say he hit a consistently harder ball than anyone ever. He could spray the ball to all fields, but because of the way he stepped into it, he hit many liners to right center. He also had enough power to smack 299 homers during his playing days.

Rajah was a good second baseman in his day, but sometimes he had trouble going back for pop flies. One reporter thought he knew why.

"Hornsby," he wrote, "was unfamiliar with pop flies because he hit so few of them himself."

The Rajah took seven batting titles during his career, but looking back at all the greatness, the one thing that has to stand out is that remarkable five-year stretch in the early '20s. That's when Rajah not only joined the .400 Club, but batted his way right to the head of the class.

In the mid- to late 1920s the era of the dead ball ended. Baseball people saw what Babe Ruth could do for the game with his many mammoth home runs, and they hopped up the ball. More players began to take the big cut and slowly forego the older style of chipping away for base hits.

There were still many great hitters around, but perhaps the knowledge that it was easier to put one out of the park took just enough off their averages to keep them out of the club. Ruth, incidentally, was a great hitter as well as a great slugger. He had a .342 lifetime average and in 1923 batted

.393, just missing the .400 mark. He didn't even win the bat crown that year, because Heilmann hit .403.

Heilmann, by the way, was another great hitter. Besides his .400 season, he won bat titles with marks of .394, .393, and .398.

Bill Terry of the New York Giants was the last National Leaguer to hit .400, with a .401 mark in 1930. Like the others, he was an outstanding hitter with a .341 lifetime mark, though he never approached .400 again. It was a hitter's year in 1930 and Terry was the best of them, gathering 254 hits to all fields. Bill almost blew it on the last day of the season. He was going after George Sisler's major league mark of 257 hits in a season, but he went hitless. Fortunately, he still made it into the club.

In 1969, someone asked Terry about another .400 hitter. Bill said, "Heavens, I certainly didn't expect to see nearly forty years go by without a .400 hitter in the National League. I thought someone would do it in a couple of years or so."

But they didn't. It was some eleven years after Terry hit .401 in 1930 before another hitter would approach the magic mark. Then it happened in the American League. The man was twenty-three-year-old Ted Williams of the Boston Red Sox.

The Splendid Splinter, as he was called, was one of the great hitters of all time. He played to the age of forty-two and was still good enough to hit .316 that year with 29 homers.

Williams' lifetime stats compare with all the other .400 hitters. His batting average over his long career was .344. He belted out 521 homers and drove in more than 1,800 runs.

He did this despite missing some five seasons because of military service. He served in World War II during 1943–1945, losing peak years. Then he was recalled during the Korean conflict and missed most of the 1952 and 1953 seasons. Had he played during those years, he would have surely set many more records and perhaps even hit .400 again. As it is, he managed a .388 average at age thirty-nine, belting 38 homers that same year of 1957.

Tall and lanky at 6-4, 200 pounds, Williams batted from the left side of the plate. He faced the pitcher straight on and ground the bat in his hands until the moment he swung. He was menacing up there. He looked like a hitter.

But it didn't all come naturally. Williams practiced and worked, then practiced some more. He weighed barely 145 pounds when he broke into pro ball and had to build himself up as well as his batting average.

"I've always done at least fifty push-ups a day," he once told a young player, then added, "and another fifty on my fingertips."

When it came to batting, Williams had even more tips. "You've got to have quick, fast hands and quick wrists. You can't let those pitchers jam you. You've got to be out in front of the ball. I've always swung a sixty-ounce bat (nearly twice the normal weight) for at least thirty minutes a day. That builds up the wrists."

Then there was practice. Williams spent countless hours in the batting cage, hitting against anyone who'd throw the ball to him. Sometimes he stayed there so long that the blisters on his hands began to bleed, but he wouldn't quit. He once said that he felt possibly only Ty Cobb might have hit more baseballs in practice than he did, adding, "I've never

Ted Williams (*Boston Red Sox*)

met a great player who didn't have to work harder at learning to play ball than anything else he ever did. But to me it was the greatest fun I've ever had."

It wasn't all easy for Ted. Often short-tempered and quick to anger, Williams often feuded with the press and sometimes with the fans. In fact, he never once tipped his cap after a home run. But he could hit.

He was also a nonconformist. He loved to wear his shirt open-necked without a tie and battled with people who just wanted him to put one on. When Joe McCarthy became manager of the Red Sox in 1948, some people anticipated a battle over the tie. But McCarthy came to his first press conference open-necked, evoking a big grin from Williams. Then the manager added:

"Any manager who can't get along with a .400 hitter is out of his mind."

The indication of Williams' greatness came early. Playing with Minneapolis in the American Association in 1938, Ted batted .366, hit 43 homers, and drove in 142 runs. As a Red Sox rookie the next year, he hit .327, poled 31 round trippers, and led the league with 145 runs batted in. The next year he hit .344. He was improving and setting the stage for the 1941 season.

It didn't look good in spring training when Ted chipped a bone in his ankle. So for the first few weeks of the season, Ted just pinch hit. He never liked the cold winds of April in Boston. Having been born in California, he much preferred the warm weather. But hitting was hitting, and Ted concentrated just as hard in any weather.

Unhappy because of the injury, Ted wanted more batting practice. He got his wish when the Sox acquired pitcher Joe Dobson from Cleveland. Dobson wasn't pitching much, and to stay in shape he volunteered to pitch batting practice to Ted. Therefore, Williams had the advantage of hitting against an active major league pitcher who was throwing hard and with good stuff.

When he got back into the lineup he was ready. Soon he was hitting everyone and hitting well. His average went up around the .400 mark and stayed there. As the season waned, people began asking the obvious question. Could Ted Williams do it? All this paved the way for one of the most dramatic days in baseball history.

Ted had actually been as high as .413 in September, but coming down to the last day of the season, a doubleheader in Philadelphia, his average was exactly .399955. Sox manager Joe Cronin told Ted he could sit out the doubleheader if he wanted to. That way his average would officially be recorded as .400 on the nose.

"No, thanks," snarled Williams, "I don't want to be a .400 hitter by my shoestrings."

As Ted stepped up to bat for the first time, umpire Bill McGowan tried to settle him down. "To hit .400 a batter has got to be loose," he said.

Then A's catcher Frank Hayes chipped in. "I wish you all the luck in the world, Ted, but we're not giving you a damn thing. Mr. Mack told us if we let up on you he'll run us out of baseball."

Now the words were over. Ted stepped in with his familiar stance, grinding the bat. He was facing right-hander Dick Fowler. He promptly slammed a single between first and second, and the crowd roared.

That hit put him officially over .400 and he could have quit then. But not Ted. He stayed in the game and the next time up pulled a Fowler fastball into the right field seats for a homer. Lefty Porter Vaughan was on the mound when Ted came up again. No difference, another single. His fourth time up produced still another hit. The Splinter was 4-for-4 in a tremendous clutch performance under pressure.

Still, Ted wouldn't quit. He insisted on playing the second game and got two more hits, including a long double. He was 6-for-8 on the day and finished the season with a .406

mark. There'd be no shoestrings for him. He was a full-fledged member of the .400 Club with no questions asked.

A long and brilliant career followed. There were the two service interruptions and several major injuries, but Ted kept playing. He won his final batting title at age forty, the oldest man ever to win a bat crown. When the time finally came for him to retire in 1960, he did it in style, belting a long home run in the final plate appearance of his career. It was as if he was saying, "I'm quitting now, but I can still swing the bat and I don't want any arguments about it."

That was the Splinter, the eighth and last member of the .400 Club.

What now? Can another player in today's game hit .400? It appears that Rod Carew of the Minnesota Twins has the greatest chance of joining the .400 Club.

At the outset of the 1977 season, Rod Carew had the highest lifetime batting average of any player in the majors, .329, and it was rising. From 1973 to 1976, Carew had batting averages of .350, .364, .359, and .332. The first three won batting titles for him. He also won the bat crown in 1969 with a .332 mark and also won in 1972 with a .318 standard.

Several times already during his career Carew has flirted with the .400 mark, only to fall off at midseason or beyond. The experts think the day might come when he doesn't fall off at all.

Rod Carew was born on October 1, 1945, in Panama's Canal Zone. He was actually born on a train which was taking his mother to a hospital.

There wasn't much money in the Carew family, but Rod didn't care. As he recalls:

"I never wanted the so-called luxury toys that other kids

had. There was just one thing that made me happy from as far back as I can remember, and that was walking around all day with a bat and glove."

Baseball was very popular in Panama, so Rod never had to look very far for the nearest game. He got plenty of practice, from Little League on up.

When Rod was sixteen his parents separated and his mother took him and his three sisters to New York. It wasn't easy for Rod. He had to learn a new language and make new friends. There was another problem. His high school, George Washington High in Manhattan, didn't have a baseball team. Rod found a sandlot team, the Cavaliers, that played their games up in the Bronx. He soon became a star for the Cavaliers. This was in 1963, about a year after he came to New York.

The father of one of his teammates was a "bird dog" for a Minnesota Twins scout, Herb Stein. He told Stein about the slender youngster from Panama and arranged a tryout. Rod had his tryout right in Yankee Stadium when the Twins came to play there. When he got to bat, he swung at everything and started hitting the ball all over the lot. The more he hit the more people came around the cage to watch. Before the Twins left town they offered Rod a contract with a small bonus.

"My head was swimming," he recalls. "I just couldn't believe it was happening to me. I was nervous, scared, but I wanted to make good."

Rod played for several minor league teams and his hitting continued to improve. Because he was still relatively new to this country, he was often homesick and had some problems understanding the humor and attitude of some teammates.

But he stuck it out and in 1967 was brought up to the Twins to stay.

His rookie year was a good one, a .292 average, 150 hits, 8 homers, and 51 RBIs. All that plus the Rookie of the Year award. The next season a knee injury slowed him up and he hit just .273 in 127 games. But in 1969 came his first bat title, a .332 average, and the promise of better things to come.

In 1970, Rod started to show his stuff. He was hitting around .370 early in the year when a collision at second base caused another knee injury, this one requiring surgery. He came back near the end of the season and in 51 games hit .366. Had it not been for the injury it would have been an outstanding year. The next season he dropped off to .307, but in 1972 took his second batting title. Then the next year he began to flirt with .400.

"My own theory of hitting is to swing the bat," Carew has said. "If the ball's around the plate, swing and make contact. It's kind of a Latin tradition. That's the way I grew up in Panama. Here a lot of guys are always looking for certain pitches in certain areas. But I hate to take a pitch. If I could be a guess hitter I'd hit .500! But I don't like to think too much about hitting. I like being up there, not guessing, just getting up there and swinging free."

Some of Rod's opponents couldn't believe there wasn't more to it than that. Said veteran slugger and now Cleveland manager Frank Robinson: "Rod swings the bat about as perfectly as anyone I've seen."

Pitcher Ken Holtzman put it this way. "Rod has an uncanny ability to move the ball around as if the bat were some kind of magic wand."

Yet one writer said this: "Although Carew persists in his

Rod Carew (*Minnesota Twins*)

claim that he is a free swinger who doesn't plot out his hits, the suspicion is growing around the league that if arbitrators demanded doubles that rolled dead exactly 385 feet from the plate, or ground balls whose big hops measured exactly eleven feet at the crest, or line drives over the pitcher's left shoulder, Carew would contrive to turn those out, too."

Rod still insisted that he couldn't always place the ball just where he wanted to. He seemed to hit to the opposite field more than pulling the ball to right. He explained that.

"Usually when I try to pull the ball I hit off my front foot and can't get anything behind on my swing. So I just concentrate on hitting up the middle or going to the opposite field."

Like Ty Cobb and Ted Williams, Carew is a firm believer in practice.

"I'm different from a lot of young hitters I see today," he said in 1975. "We had a day off Monday and I took ten extra minutes of batting practice on Tuesday. I take all the extra batting practice I can get. Guys who are hitting .190 and .220 should be doing that, and they don't. They should be asking questions, and they don't. It's a funny thing about ball players. They get to the big leagues and they stop trying to learn; they don't think they have to improve anymore. I've tried to tell some guys about things they're doing wrong. But they just keep doing them over and over again."

Whenever Rod feels he has a weakness, he works to improve it. One time he was having trouble with high, inside fastballs. He went right to work and overcame it.

"A guy has to know what kind of a hitter he is and has to know his limits. I've seen guys who make an out come back and break their bats and helmets. The pitchers are getting paid to get you out. I always had the attitude that if a guy gets me today, I'll get him tomorrow."

Does it all sound familiar? It's the same kind of attitude that the older players had, an attitude that is often missing in today's high-salaried game. There's something else that Rod does better than anyone in baseball today, another throwback to earlier times. He's an expert bunter. In fact, he'd gotten up to twenty-nine bunt hits a year, and that can really boost the old average.

"Even when they know I'm going to bunt they can't always throw me out," he says. "I can drop the ball to a spot where they will have an awkward throw. They have to come up clean with the ball and throw on the run. Not too many third basemen can do that all the time."

During spring training Rod will practice his bunting some forty-five minutes a day, and even during the season he spends about fifteen minutes before each game dropping them down. After bunting, he practices spraying the ball to all fields and at varying distances from home plate.

"All some of these guys want to do in batting practice is put the ball in the seats," says Rod. "I concentrate on moving it around."

It's no wonder that Carew is today's best hitter. In 1974 he got the .400 people talking for the first time. In a game in late June he went hitless against the Orioles and his average dropped below .400 for the first time. But he made some adjustments in his swing and got two hits the next night to get back up there.

"If Rod gets lucky and stays healthy, I think he can hit .400," says Twins manager Frank Quilicy. "He has so many offensive gifts. And when he isn't hitting he can always bunt for hits."

Rod himself didn't really want to talk about it.

"When you set goals you add pressure," he said, "and there's enough of that already. But you know, I'm pretty much of a free swinger and I don't walk too much. I think I walked 62 times in 1973. Ted Williams had something like 145 walks when he hit .406. And now, with so many good relief pitchers around, you're always facing somebody fresh. Every team has three or four good starters and a couple of very good relievers. That's a lot of pitching."

That part was true. Rod tailed off in July and August and finished the year with a .364 mark. But he showed there were possibilities that it could be done again.

For the first month and a half of 1975 Rod was hitting .346, leading the league as usual. But then he got hot. In a three-game series against the Yanks he had 12 hits in 13 times at bat. He extended that to 26 for 42, a .619 clip; then 35 for 59, a .593 surge. Overall it raised his season's mark to .425 and the .400 talk started all over again. The big streak really gave Rod confidence.

"The last ten days I've felt so confident that I think there's not a pitcher around who can get me out. I really don't think anyone can hit better than me."

Now the writers were looking to the old .400 hitters. One found a statement made by Ty Cobb back in 1960. "Somebody will hit .400 again," Tyrus said. "Somebody will get smart and swing naturally."

Bill Terry put it this way. "To hit .400 you need a great start, and you can't have a slip. Hitting is a business. With two strikes you really got to protect that plate."

And Ted Williams added: "To hit .400 you've got to have power to keep the defense back and spread out. And you've got to be fast."

Now more players than ever were praising Carew. The prevailing opinion seemed to be that he could put the ball pretty much where he wanted to. The reporters flocked to Carew, asking him about a .400 season.

"It's too early to say now," he admitted. "But if I'm hitting .385 at the end of August or in early September, then I think I might be able to do it. Last year it got to a point where I thought I might do it, so now I'm trying not to think about it."

Some minor injuries, muscle pulls, kept him out of several games the second half of the season. This, too, might have been a factor. For he slowly tailed off once more and finished at .359. Still, he had given it a run and left the door open.

Rod is playing more first base now, rather than second. That could eliminate some wear and tear on his legs. But he takes care of himself. In nice weather he often makes the thirty mile trip to and from the ball park on a bicycle, rather than by car. That's the kind of thing they used to do way back when.

Whether or not Rod Carew ever hits .400 isn't really the important thing. He has already shown he can do it, that he has the equipment if all other conditions are right. What is important is that Rod Carew, and some others, are once again playing baseball the way it was played many years ago.

Others will follow in the same tradition. If not Carew, then perhaps some other player will come along to hit .400. After all, that club needs some new members before it's too late.

CHAPTER 3

Thieves

To do it right, you've got to be more than fast. You've got to be quick and smart. You've got to study and observe. You've got to have instinct and an inner voice that says, GO!

If you haven't guessed by now, the subject is the ancient art of base stealing, thievery on the diamond, a maneuver that can spell the difference between winning and losing. Stealing was once an integral part of baseball strategy. Take a look at the league-leading numbers around 1910, and the years just before and after. For both leagues they read: 61, 53, 70, 80, 76, 81, 88, 96. That's just a random sampling.

With the advent of the home run in the middle 1920s, the stolen base became less a part of the game. Except for the occasional appearance of a superthief, the numbers were much lower. In the early 1930s guys were leading the league with the likes of 28, 20, 27 steals. It didn't get much better.

In 1950, the American League leader had 15 stolen bases. Two years later the American had a 22-stolen-base man, while the National boasted a 30-steal king. Sure, these are just numbers, maybe meaningless ones. But it does point up the fact that the stolen base, one of baseball's more exciting plays, all but disappeared from the scene for a period of some thirty years.

Beginning in the late 1950s, the stolen base began to reappear as an effective offensive weapon. Through the 1960s and into the '70s the trend has continued, with many of today's players running with the same kind of abandon as in the past.

True, there aren't as many opportunities to run today as in, say, 1910. But there are a good number of players who can and will run when given the chance, and they're quite good at it.

Some of the outstanding base stealers of the mid-1970s include Davey Lopes, Joe Morgan, Bert Campaneris, Rod Carew, Amos Otis, Cesar Cedeno, and Mickey Rivers. However, there's a name missing, a very important name. The *King* has been left out, a man many consider the best base stealer of all time. He's Lou Brock of the St. Louis Cardinals, who will undoubtedly end his career with nearly every major stolen base record in his corner.

Brock has been a great base stealer with the St. Louis Cardinals for years. It was his consistency more than anything else that amazed everyone. In 1965, Lou's fourth season in the majors, he swiped 63 bases. He's never been under 50 steals since, setting a record with twelve straight years of 50 steals or more through 1976.

The big one was in 1974, when at the age of thirty-five, Lou Brock swiped the amazing total of 118 bases in 153 games. Considering his age and the wear and tear of base stealing, it had to be one of the greatest records of all time.

There's even more significance to Lou's record, however, because in a sense it provides the final link in a chain of baseball thieves; a chain which, in effect, traces the history of the stolen base in the national pastime.

Brock's 118 steals broke a record set just a dozen years earlier in 1962. That's when Maury Wills of the Los Angeles Dodgers pilfered 104 bases. The significance of Wills' feat, besides being of record-breaking proportions, was that it heralded the return of the stolen base as a major offensive weapon.

Whose record did Wills break? Now we go back a long time, for Maury cracked a record that was set way back in 1915. This record of 96 steals was set by none other than the Georgia Peach, the great Tyrus Raymond "Ty" Cobb.

Cobb's mark came in the heyday of the steal, when many runners were trying to take that extra ninety feet for free. As usual, Ty wouldn't settle for anything less than being the best. After Ty and his cohorts left the game, the stolen base all but retired until Wills came along to put it back on the map. That's why the Cobb-Wills-Brock chain is so important.

The other interesting thing is the contrasting styles of the three thieves. All had entirely different ways of operating on the basepaths, yet all were equally successful. Let's look at these three superthieves and the way they worked their magic on the diamond.

Much of the Ty Cobb story is already known. Often considered baseball's greatest hitter, Ty had a lifetime average of .367 for twenty-three years and an all-time high of 4,191 hits. He'd do just about anything to get on base, so it's no wonder that he'd do just about anything to steal one.

Ty's early days in the game were rough. When he first

joined the Detroit Tigers in 1905, he took a terrific hazing from veteran teammates who didn't want to see the youngster put one of their friends out of a job. They even went so far as to vow to drive Ty off the team. But Cobb fought back, with his fists and with his play. The entire incident, which didn't end until the other players realized they might lose a superstar, probably helped make Ty the kind of ball player he became. As he himself said:

"From then on a terrible anger was in me. Anger, hatred, and humiliation. I hadn't been raised to brawl like this. I didn't see why ball players should lower themselves to an animal level. The one and only way I could see to settle the clique's hash was to out-hustle, and if possible, outplay all members of the anti-Cobb faction. And to do this I bore down with everything I had."

Cobb became a hustler and competitor supreme, and the stolen base quickly became part of his arsenal. As the years passed, Ty learned more and more tricks on the basepaths. The first thing he learned was to abandon the headfirst slide he had always used. This maneuver is used somewhat today, notably by Pete Rose of the Reds, but Ty learned as a rookie that you couldn't get away with it in those days.

Early in his rookie season he banged out a hit and tried to stretch it into a double. A shortstop named Kid Elberfeld was waiting at second. Ty came in headfirst. Not only did Elberfeld slam the ball into Ty's head, but for good measure he brought his knee down on the back of the rookie's neck, grinding Ty's face into the dirt. That's the way the game was played then, especially when dealing with a rookie.

Ty wasn't the type to be intimidated. The next time he came into second against Elberfeld, he did it feet first and

Ty Cobb (*Detroit Tigers*)

sent the shortstop sprawling toward left field. Elberfeld got up, brushed himself off, smiled, and said:

"That's how it's done, kid. You've got it now and more power to you."

So Cobb earned respect, and before long that respect in the eyes of many turned to fear. For Ty Cobb on the base paths was truly a man to be reckoned with.

Ty's basic philosophy was to keep them throwing. The more you made them throw the ball around, the more likely they'd make a mistake. He readily admitted there were faster players (though he was no slouch) who couldn't steal as well. He claimed that stealing bases was nearly 90 percent mental.

"My whole plan was to upset infields and batteries [pitcher and catcher]," he said. "I did it by dividing their minds, by upsetting and worrying them until their concentration slipped. I always looked to create a mental error and many times I did."

Cobb would surely steal to get his team another run or to win a game. But he also used the basepaths to settle personal scores, or to humiliate someone who was taking too many liberties with him or his teammates. For instance, the Red Sox had a catcher named Lou Criger who apparently had been tossing anti-Cobb jargon all around the league, claiming that Ty was all talk and no action and couldn't really produce on the paths. Naturally, Ty burned and planned to get even. He waited until the first Boston-Detroit series of 1908. The great Cy Young was on the mound for the Red Sox as Ty came up for the first time. Suddenly, he turned around toward Criger and said:

"I'm gonna steal every base on you today."

Then he promptly singled. Ty took a big lead, but Young threw to first, driving him back. After a few more throws, Ty yelled at Criger again.

"I'm going down on the next pitch!"

Sure enough, as soon as Young kicked, Ty took off, and he slid safely into second by a wide margin. He then growled at Criger again.

"This time I'm going to third, you big baboon, on the next pitch."

With Criger burning mad, Ty got another big lead and took off. Once again he was in safely ahead of Criger's throw. But he wasn't finished.

"Now on the next one I'm coming home, ice wagon," he shouted.

Bursting down the line, Ty came in feet first. He banged hard into Criger and was called safe by the umpire. He had done it—he had come around from first on just four pitches. After that, Criger kept his mouth shut and Ty never had trouble stealing on him again. Years later Ty told how he did it.

"The secret was Cy Young," said Ty. "It took me a while to find his weak spot, but I did. He not only had a slow windup, but he tipped off the times he was going to throw to first. Some pitchers will lob the ball over, then fire one to catch you off guard. Young threw hard to first base all the time. But he only threw over when his elbows were slightly away from his body. When he tucked them in, I knew he would pitch to the plate.

"Then by announcing my intentions to Criger, I just increased the pressure on him. He was shocked when I made second. Then he didn't believe me when I told him I'd go to third. But as soon as I saw Young's elbows in close I could call my shot. I had him furious and panicky, not knowing how I got such a big jump on his pitcher."

Ty had all kinds of tricks. He singled in the 1907 World Series against the Cubs. When the next hitter singled to right he took off. As he neared the base he saw the right-fielder making his throw. He could also see that second baseman Johnny Evers didn't know where shortstop Joe Tinker was standing. When Evers got the ball, he heard someone shout, "Tag him!" and he figured it was Tinker. He lunged at the bag with his glove, but no one was there. Ty had already rounded the bag and was heading for third, where he slid in safely. Once more, Ty explained.

"I knew that Evers couldn't see Tinker and that if I hollered 'Tag him!' he'd figure Tinker was yelling. Then, when no one was there, he was thinking of Tinker, wondering why Joe yelled at him. And the split second he took to think about it gave me time to make it into third. It just didn't dawn on him that the voice he heard was mine. Sometimes a little suggestion can go a long way."

There were times when Ty would spend months, even years, setting a player up for the one time he could take advantage of him. He related how in 1911 he spent most of the season creating a conditioned reflex in all-star first baseman Hal Chase. Whenever Ty was on second and a ball was hit to Chase, Ty would round third by ten or twelve feet. Chase would make the putout at first and then fire hard to third, where Ty would just get back to the bag in time.

"It became a routine thing," said Ty. "We'd grin at each other when it happened. Neither of us gained a thing, that is, until the day I didn't stop. It was the same play. Chase made his usual throw to third and the third baseman started to apply the tag. Only I was streaking toward home, cutting the plate before he could recover and throw. It was one run in one game, and it wouldn't happen the same way again. But, believe me, it was well worth all the time I took to set it up."

Ty would sometimes arrive in a city early, and instead of drinking beer or playing cards with his teammates, he'd look up old retired ball players and talk to them, admitting he was "picking their brains," looking for any edge he might find.

Other times he'd fake an injury, like a twisted knee or ankle, when he got on base. Sometimes he'd even roll around on the ground as if in great pain. Then he'd attempt to shake it off, as if he were gallantly trying to stay in the game. But on the very next pitch he'd be off, leaving his opponents cursing in his wake. As Ty said:

"Little white lies can make big black numbers on the scoreboard for your team, if you've first set the stage for them."

Ty the actor was also Ty the perfectionist. He'd work on fundamentals by the hour, sometimes just running the bases and practicing his turns. Oftentimes he'd slide until his body ached and his skin was rubbed raw. Sliding was very important to him.

"The whole secret of sliding is to make your move at the last possible second," he once said. "If you leave your feet too soon you lose your mobility. When I went in there I wanted to see the whites of the fielder's eyes. I liked to come straight at him, then collapse to the right or left after faking the other way.

"Sometimes I'd deliberately slide wide, go past the bag, then reach back and hook the outside corner with my trailing toe. Or sometimes I'd go even further past and reach back with my hand to get the bag. Five fingers isn't much to give a defensive man who has to catch the ball and put it on you in the same motion."

Ty reached his zenith with 96 steals in 1915. It wasn't easy. Playing on rough, unkempt infields, Ty's body took a tremendous beating. He was bruised, battered, and exhausted by the time the season ended, but that's the way he played the game.

There were some other big stealing years for Ty. He had 83 one year, 76 another, and 68 another. In all, he led the league six times, proving there were other fine thiefs around, too. When he hung his spikes up in 1928, he had swiped 892 sacks, a record that has stood for nearly half a century. However, at the outset of the 1977 season, Lou Brock was just some 30 steals away.

Before looking at Brock, let's go back to Maury Wills, the great Dodger shortstop of the 1960s. Maury came to the majors late in life. He was almost twenty-eight when he became a Dodger rookie in 1959. In the seven years before that, no American League player had stolen as many as 30 bases in a season, while the best the National could do in that period were 40 and 38 by Willie Mays.

Wills came along at a time when stolen bases were still way down the list of offensive weapons. Maury wasn't a big man, about 5-10 and 165 pounds, and probably a lot lighter by August and September of each year. He was a switch hitter, though, who got on base quite often and usually batted in the lead-off spot.

Maury showed his stuff early. In 1960, his second year in the league, he swiped 50 bags to win the league crown. The next year he took it again, but only with 35 steals. Then in

1962 he started running early and often. He swiped base after base, and before long people were beginning to talk about Cobb's record. Records were certainly in the air then. Just a year earlier Roger Maris had belted 61 homers to top the Babe, so fans everywhere were pumped up by record-breaking.

Like Cobb, Wills was a fiery competitor who played it hard all the way. His opponents were his enemies and he tried every trick in the book to outfox them. He rarely talked to members of the other team, as one National League first baseman testified.

"Maury was always very intense. When he got on base he'd never talk to you. He was too busy concentrating on his lead and the pitcher. By contrast, Brock is different. He'll give you a cheery hello, then take his lead. But they were the same in one way. *Woooooosh*, and they're both gone."

Wills was like Cobb in yet another way. He believed that much of baseball was mental, and you could use psychological warfare to your advantage.

"I've always said it was possible to condition an umpire to react in your favor," Wills once said. "But you can't do it by chatting with him, or being friendly, or bribing him with a glove or bat for his kid. You condition an umpire by hustling. Say you hit a grounder to the infield. You know you don't have a chance, but you bust your butt going down the line just the same and are thrown out by five feet. The next time you do it, the same thing happens and you're thrown out by three feet. Finally there comes the close play—bang, bang—and the umpire calls you safe. The reason is that he saw you really putting out the first two times and he's already thinking in your favor. He's conditioned and you get the nod."

Maury Wills (*Baseball Hall of Fame*)

Maury feels he proved this by his base stealing. "On almost every close play in the years I was stealing a lot of bases, I was called safe. Even when the ump wasn't in position to really see it, I was called safe without a moment's hesitation.

"But later in my career things changed. I wasn't stealing as much and on close plays I was often called out, even when I knew the shortstop or second baseman missed me. They were the identical plays that saw me safe in earlier years. One time I asked an ump why, reminding him that he used to call me safe on the same play. 'Well, Maury,' he answered, 'you aren't stealing the way you used to.' "

As Cobb once said, a little suggestion can go a long way. Wills has more evidence of that very thing.

"There was a time when I stole the 104 that I ran on the Cubs. I don't think they threw me out all year. Anyway, as I started my slide, I heard the ump already calling me safe. I must have been five feet from the bag. When the Cub shortstop complained, the umpire said, 'Look, you haven't got Wills out all year. What makes you think you're going to get him now?'

"This is conditioning. The ump can't always be in perfect position to see the play, so the good base stealer is going to get the benefit of the doubt. The umpires, like the fans and players, expect him to make it."

Again like Cobb, Wills used a variety of slides. They often left his body battered and beaten. But in 1962 he kept running, even with the pressure of the record and a tight pennant race beside him. He did it, cracking Cobb's old mark and setting a new standard of 104 steals.

Perhaps it was the battering, but Wills didn't run as much the following year, stealing just 40 sacks. In 1965 he had another big year, with 94 steals. Then the same thing happened. In '66 he was limited to just 38. The big years seemed to take something out of him.

Since Ty Cobb had died in 1961, he didn't see Wills approach and then break his record in 1962. There's no way of knowing how the Georgia Peach would have reacted. But when Brock started chasing Wills' mark, Maury was right there watching. He was honest enough to admit his feelings.

"I never thought anyone would approach the record so soon," Maury said. "I felt it was my record and I was very proud of it. It was very much a part of me, a part of my identification, and I didn't think anyone would top it in my lifetime. I'm not even going to say that records are made to be broken. It would be very wishy-washy of me to say that. In fact, I don't think anyone looks forward to seeing his own record broken."

A competitor like Wills probably wished he could get out there and go head to head with Brock. Of course, he couldn't.

"I started having mixed emotions when Lou went over the 70 mark," said Wills. "I was really hoping he wouldn't do it, but when he went over 80 it became rather obvious. The one thing I never wished on him was any kind of tough luck. My hat's off to him, believe me."

Maury Wills is an honest person and a class guy.

Oddly enough, it may have been Wills, who, in an indirect kind of way, helped boost Brock to his record-breaking effort. It happened at the beginning of the 1973 season. Lou had already stolen his 50 or more bases for eight straight years, but suddenly he wasn't running well. He had been thrown out 13 of the first 23 times he ran.

"I was getting all kinds of negative vibes running through my head," he recalls. "I was almost thirty-four years old and

I was beginning to believe I was slowing up. I remember one day I was stealing and I just stopped, right in the middle of the baseline and for no reason. I was a sitting duck."

That's when Lou ran into Wills. "Maury didn't beat around the bush. He knew what was troubling me and told me to keep running. The big thing, he said, was not to start counting the times I was caught. Soon I was running well again and I had my confidence back. I'll always thank him for that."

Lou finished the season with 70 steals, the second best mark of his career. Still, no one—not even Lou—expected what would happen the next year. In fact, when he first came to the majors as a Chicago Cub in 1962, the year of Wills' record, Lou wasn't even a base thief. His chief concern up to that time was simply getting to the majors and staying there.

Lou Brock was born on June 18, 1939, in El Dorado, Arkansas, but he grew up in Mer Rouge, Louisiana. Lou was one of nine children, and there wasn't much money, so growing up wasn't very easy. Being black and poor in a small town made the real world a distant and strange place.

"I didn't know there was such a thing as a steady job when I was young," says Lou. "I thought everybody had a job for a day or two, then got another one."

There were many unpleasant memories for Lou. Even when he and his friends played ball, they did it without much enthusiasm. There just wasn't anything to motivate them. Then, while in grade school, Lou was caught throwing a spitball. As punishment, he was sent to the library to look up information on the careers of Jackie Robinson, Don Newcombe, Stan Musial, and Joe DiMaggio.

Lou was impressed by their achievements, but he was

impressed even more by the amount of money they made. To him, Joe D's $100,000 contract was like all the money in the world. From that day on he decided to be a ball player.

After an outstanding high school career, Lou went to Southern University, an all-black school in Baton Rouge. The year was 1958 and he still had a lot to learn about the game. The next year he came on, hitting .542 and making all-conference. By 1961 the Chicago Cubs offered the young outfielder a $30,000 bonus to sign with them. He saw the dollar signs and signed the contract.

He had a great minor league season in '61, hitting .361, and the next year was up with the Cubs. It was a rapid rise, but Lou had worked hard for it. As a rookie, he got into 123 games, batting .263 with 114 hits, 9 homers, and 35 RBIs. He also stole 16 bases, but he did it mainly with speed and didn't consider it a real part of his game.

The next year Lou was a regular, but his stats were pretty much the same—a .258 average, 9 homers, and 37 ribbys. He stole 24 bases, but also struck out 122 times. When Lou still showed no real improvement in the early weeks of '64, he was worried. Something had to give.

Then, on June 15, Lou got the word. He had been traded to the St. Louis Cardinals for Ernie Broglio, a former twenty-game winner. When Lou reached St. Louis he was told he was the regular leftfielder and was installed in the second spot in the batting order. He's been a star ever since.

Lou caught fire as soon as he joined his new team. The Cards were in a pennant race and Lou responded. One reason was a decision he had reached.

"When I first came to the majors I thought power hitting was where the money was. But I realized I didn't have consistent power. So I had to make a choice. Do I go and try to

Lou Brock (*St. Louis Cardinals*)

develop myself as a powerhitter, or do I become a pest on the basepaths?

"I made the final decision when I was traded to the Cards. I looked at myself all over again. That's when I became a baserunner."

Lou was a .300 hitter from the day he joined the Cards. He hit .348 after he went over and .315 for the season. He also cracked out 200 hits and drove in 58 runs. His steals were up to 43 and he began to work hard on his thievery.

With Brock in left, the Cards won the pennant. They also won the World Series that year, with Lou hitting .300 again. He was always tough when the chips were down. When the Cards got into World Series play in 1967 and 1968, Lou had 12 and 13 hits and batting averages of .414 and .464. He also swiped 7 bases in each series.

Lou became a master of base stealing the next two years, getting 63 and 74. With Maury Wills getting old, Brock was the new superstar of the basepaths.

As far as his style is concerned, Lou's is markedly different from Cobb's and Wills'. First of all, Lou is not the outwardly intense competitor that they were. The fires obviously burn, but they burn within. Lou will talk to the fielders, not to distract them, but because he is friendly. However, he always has enough control to know just what he's doing out there.

Secondly, while Cobb and Wills had a variety of slides and ways of getting to the base, Lou always does it the same way, straight in. He believes the shortest distance from one point to another is a straight line.

"I saw Maury Wills run quite often," Lou said. "He used the hook slide almost exclusively. That means he's always going for the corner of the base. It's a beautiful, but damaging slide, because a larger portion of your body—legs, rump, arms, elbows, and even back—can make contact with the ground. I always use the straight-in, or 'pop-up' slide. That way, just my calves absorb any real contact or punishment."

The pop-up is just as it sounds. Lou slides, and in one motion is back on his feet, usually before the ump can give the safe call. But there's more to it than that.

"Speed isn't everything," says Lou. "I've seen plenty of guys faster than me who can't run the bases. And it isn't the element of surprise, either. If I depended on surprise, I'd steal just 25 or 30 bases a year.

"It's been years of practice and torture for me," Lou continued. "First of all, it's learning to read the pitchers. Every baserunner must do this if he expects to steal successfully. By reading the pitcher the runner knows when to run and when he can get his best jump. This is all related to leading, to know just how far you can get off and still get back. Then there's the initial thrust. A player can practice this. But he must be running at top speed within ten steps or so.

"When I get on base, no matter what the situation, I always think about the same things—the catcher's strengths and limitations and reading the pitcher. At the same time they're reading me. All of them know I'm gonna go. That's one of the keys to successful base stealing, making them aware that I'm a threat.

"I want them to concentrate on me. My tactic is to force the issue, to put it to the other guy. Then he becomes anxious. He wants to make the perfect play, and once I've got him trying that, I've beaten him."

Both Brock and Maury Wills agree on something else. It was more difficult stealing 100 bases in 1974 than it was in 1962.

"In some ways the record was more difficult for Lou than it was for me," said Wills. "At the time I broke Cobb's mark everyone was home-run conscious, and the pitchers weren't used to keeping runners close to first. I could get some pretty good leads. But after I broke the record things kind of changed. Pitchers started working to keep the good runners close so they wouldn't get that huge jump."

Lou's comparison deals with the catchers. "When I first came up," he says, "there just wasn't that much stealing and the catchers weren't ready. Not that many of them could get the ball down to second quickly, and not many of their throws came in low and on the bag. But with more players running in the last years, the young catchers are ready. They can all throw and welcome the challenge of cutting down the top runners."

Lou was running well at the beginning of 1974 and hitting well. By the time the team had played 56 games, about one-third of the season, he had already stolen 40 bases. Talk of a record run started. When questioned about his steals, Lou told one reporter he just didn't like first base.

"First base is nowhere," he said, "and most times it's useless to stay there. On the other hand, second base is probably the safest place on the field. When I steal second, I practically eliminate the double play, and I can score on almost anything hit past the infield."

When the team had completed half its schedule, Lou had 50 steals. On August 1, he had 66. It seemed the pace was slowing. Many people said they knew it, that at age thirty-five Lou couldn't possibly keep up the pace in the hot summer months. But then came a weekend series against Philadelphia, and Lou swiped eight bases in nine tries. The record talk began all over again.

Lou got steal number 90 in the team's 113th game. Now it looked as if only an injury could stop him. Then, in early September, there was a new threat. Both Lou and rookie outfielder Bake McBride received a death threat from a man who claimed he was terminally ill and had nothing to live for. He said he was going to shoot them right at the ball park. There was extra police protection, but the two players were edgy.

"I can't say this doesn't bother me," said Lou. "Whenever someone threatens to kill you it's real, the fear is there. Both Bake and I have got to try to forget about it."

Fortunately, nothing ever happened, and Lou kept right on running. He got steal number 100 against the Mets on September 6. Then on the night of September 10, he tied and broke the old record against Philadelphia. The game was stopped and Lou was honored right there on the field. He was given the base as a memento. Afterwards, he faced reporters.

"I never thought it would happen," he admitted, "but now that it did I'm glad it's over. I can't really say I care about records because I'm not on an ego trip. I just steal to win. But maybe when I'm seventy-five I'll care."

Lou was telling the truth about winning. The Cards were in the pennant race and that's what he really wanted. He kept running and got his record up to 118 by season's end. Unfortunately, the team fell a bit short. One writer dwelled on this when writing about Lou's achievement.

"The shame of it is," wrote the man, "that the Cards didn't win the pennant. Because then the entire country would have had the pleasure of seeing Lou Brock perform in another World Series, where his sheer artistry becomes more evident than ever."

Fortunately, Lou kept going. He showed that his 5-11, 175-pound body could take it. In 1975 he swiped 56 bases in 136 games while hitting .309. In '76, at the age of thirty-seven, he pilfered 56 more in 133 games, while hitting .301. That gave him 865 steals, just 27 short of Cobb's lifetime total. On August 29, 1977, Lou Brock swiped two bases against the San Diego Padres. They were the 892nd and 893rd of his great career, breaking Cobb's lifetime mark. Lou was now truly king of the basepaths.

It's hard to say whether Brock's record will ever be broken. There's certainly a good possibility that someone will crack it someday. Thanks to Wills and then Brock, the running game has come back to baseball, and chances are it's back to stay. People are much less likely now to forget the three great base thieves who played the game: Ty Cobb, Maury Wills, and Lou Brock.

CHAPTER 4

In Pursuit of the Babe and Other Home Run Sluggers

There have been a score of great and very great baseball players down through the years. To pick the best this and the best that from those players is just about impossible. When you want to pick the one player whose name is most closely associated with the game of baseball, though, it's easy. For this man is a legend and will never be forgotten. In a sense, he's already become part of America's folklore. He is George Herman Ruth, the wonderful Babe.

It's difficult to find a finer all-around player. The Babe was an outstanding major league pitcher, a two-time twenty-game winner, before he became the Sultan of Swat, the Bambino, the man who could hit a baseball farther than anyone.

Yet Babe isn't always remembered as a great all-around player. He's remembered more for his flamboyant personality, his zest for living, and some of his legendary exploits, both on and off the diamond.

He's also remembered for his home runs—but not for how

many times he led the league, or how many runs his circuits drove in, or how many games they won. That all counts, of course, but when most people think of the Babe and his homers, they think of two marks which he created during his career. The first is his season record of 60 homers, and the second his career standard of 714 four baggers.

Both were mighty records which stood the onslaught of many strong, determined sluggers. The pursuit of the Babe was always one of baseball's most talked-about topics. Most people felt that one year someone could get hot and topple the 60 mark. But almost no one figured that any player could stay around long enough and be consistent enough to erase the 714.

Then it happened. In 1961 another New York Yankee outfielder, Roger Maris, got in a groove and stayed there all year. He did the impossible by belting out 61 home runs during the season. His achievement was somewhat tempered by an elongated 162 game season (compared to the Babe's 154), and there's an asterisk noting such next to his name in the record book. Still, the 714 looked safe.

Then in the 1950s and '60s a whole new group of sluggers began belting out homers. Would one of them have a chance at the 714? There were Mickey Mantle and Willie Mays, Ernie Banks and Eddie Mathews, Harmon Killebrew, and Frank Robinson. There was also Henry Aaron. One by one these great sluggers came on, threatened the mark, then faded, retired, and came up short. All went over 500 homers, while Mays went over 600.

One man didn't fade. Henry Aaron kept playing and kept hitting home runs. He never had that real big season, but his consistency was amazing. He was usually somewhere in the middle-40s when each season ended. One by one he passed the other sluggers in career homers. Then he began the final assault on the Babe.

On April 8, 1974, Henry ended all suspense by belting his 715th homer. He was the new king. While his accomplishments (homers weren't the only ones) didn't diminish the Ruth legend, Hammerin' Hank went on to hit 755 homers before he retired. He was the bona fide new champ, and he left no doubt about it.

There have been many great records set in the long history of the game of baseball, but the home run seems to hold the most fascination for the largest number of people. Let's see how the mighty Babe came to set his records and how they finally fell.

The timing of the Babe's rise couldn't have been better. Born in Baltimore, Maryland, on February 6, 1895, George Herman Ruth spent his early years living above his father's saloon in a pretty tough section of the city. He learned street language and street activities while he was quite young. It wasn't a good atmosphere for a youngster to grow in.

When he was seven, the Babe's parents decided to send him to the St. Mary's Industrial School for Boys. As Babe himself described it, St. Mary's was, ". . . a training school for orphans, incorrigibles, delinquents, boys whose homes had been broken by divorce, runaways picked up on the streets, and children of poor parents who had no other means of providing an education for them. I was listed as an incorrigible and I guess I was."

Babe spent the better part of the next nine years at St. Mary's, and it was there that he learned to play baseball. His primary teacher was one of the Xaverian Brothers who ran the school, Brother Matthias, whom the Babe always referred to as "the greatest man I've ever known."

Lou Gehrig (*New York Yankees*)

Babe became a star left-handed pitcher at St. Mary's, claiming that he immediately "felt a strange relationship with the pitcher's mound. It was as if I'd been born out there. Pitching just felt like the most natural thing in the world. Striking out batters was easy."

In 1914, when Babe was just eighteen, he was discovered by Jack Dunn, manager of the International League's Baltimore Orioles. He signed Babe to a contract and even became his legal guardian. Once into pro ball it didn't take Babe long. Before the season was out he took his 22-9 record at Baltimore right to the majors with the Boston Red Sox. A year later, 1915, he was winning eighteen games for the Sox, and in the next two years had marks of 23-12 and 24-13. He pitched in the World Series of 1916 and 1918, winning three and losing none, and setting a Series record of twenty-nine straight scoreless innings which was to stand for many years.

While it seemed the Babe was on the brink of becoming a superpitcher, the Sox also noticed that he could belt the ball a country mile. His batting average was always over .300, and on days he wasn't pitching, the Sox began using him in the outfield. By 1918 he was playing more in the outfield than pitching. He threw just 166 innings and had a 13-7 mark, while he came to bat 317 times, tied for the league lead in homers with 11, and batted .300. The next year he pitched even less (9-5 and still a winner), while batting .322, setting a new record for homers with 29, and leading the league in RBIs with 112. He was good.

Now the Sox had to decide what to do with the big guy. The team had a new owner and the man was in debt. He needed money and the best way to get it was to sell some of his star players. The owners of the New York Yankees were friends of his, so it was easy to make a deal. Before the 1920

Babe Ruth (*New York Yankees*)

season, the Babe was sold to the New York Yankees for $125,000.

Once in New York the Babe commenced to be a full-time outfielder and continued to break records. Baseball had suffered a tremendous loss of prestige when it was learned that several members of the 1919 Chicago White Sox had taken money from gamblers to throw the World Series. This was the infamous Black Sox Scandal, and many thought the game of baseball would never recover from this.

What people didn't count on was the attractiveness of Babe Ruth. The big guy, who stood 6-2 and weighed 215 pounds and up, really rocked things in 1920 with 54 home runs, 137 RBIs and a .376 batting average. He was still hitting in the era of the dead ball and a homer mark like that was unbelievable. People began flocking to ball parks wherever the Yankees played. The Babe was a character and a great player.

His off-field exploits were constantly in the papers. Here was a man who never had money in his life. Now he had plenty, and he was spreading it around like butter on bread. The Babe loved to eat and drink and party all night. He'd leave a hundred dollar tip as if it were a dime. He'd sometimes overeat and drink too much, and he tangled with his manager. Yet he continued to play and bash home runs.

In 1921 he proved that his hitting and his homers were no fluke. He belted 59 of the big ones, hit .378, and whacked home 170 runs. The Yankees were building a powerhouse team and the Babe was the central figure, the man everyone wanted to see. He was the most popular and dynamic player in baseball.

By 1927, the Yankees had the greatest team in baseball, a star-studded cast of characters that some call the greatest of all time. The team also had another great slugger, Lou Gehrig, who blasted his share of homers, though he was more of a line drive hitter than the Babe. In 1927 the two of them began hitting homers from the first of the year. While the Yanks pulled away from the rest of the American League, interest centered on Ruth and Gehrig. Who would hit the most home runs?

The two sluggers stayed pretty close until September. Then the Babe went on a tear that saw him clobber 17 more home runs. The final one came off Tom Zachery of Washington on the last day of the season. It was the Babe's 60th home run of the season, a new record. Gehrig, by the way, finished with 47. The Yanks won 110 games to romp in the World Series against Pittsburgh. Babe remembers how it was before the Series began.

"The Pirates took batting practice first. It was down at Forbes Field in Pittsburgh. Most of them hadn't seen us before, so they hung around to watch. That was their mistake.

"Our practice pitcher was just grooving them and Lou and I banged ball after ball into the right-field stands. I finally blasted one right out of the park in center. Then Bob Meusel and Tony Lazzeri came up and started hammering balls into the left-field stands the same way. One by one the Pirate players got up and left the park, many of them shaking their heads in disbelief."

The Series was over before it began. The Yanks won in four games.

The rest of the Ruth story is well known. Babe never really took care of himself. He got heavy and was ill several times. His great natural skills, however, kept him in the game some 22 years and kept him hitting homers. In 1934, at

Jimmie Fox (*Baseball Hall of Fame*)

age thirty-nine, he still managed to hit 22, but he was just about through. The Yanks traded him to the Boston Braves, where he appeared in just 28 games in 1935 before retiring. He hit six more homers, three in one game, to finish with 714.

Babe was not always a happy man in retirement. He yearned to get back into baseball, to manage the Yankees, but he had been so unreliable as a player as far as discipline and his personal habits were concerned, that the club didn't want to take a chance on him. He died early, at the age of fifty-three, in 1948, a victim of cancer. Yet his legend and his two standards of 60 homers in a season and 714 homers kept his name on the lips of baseball fans always.

The first real challenge to Babe's 60 homers came in 1932. The hitter was Jimmy Foxx, the Maryland Strong Boy, a Hall of Famer and great home run hitter. By July, Foxx was over 40 homers and it looked as if he might break the mark. Babe was still active then, in fact, and had 41 homers that season. He watched Foxx approach his mark.

A wrist injury slowed old Double X in August, but in September he started his final assault. Foxx came up short though, finishing with 58 home runs. Yet there's more to the story than that. With a little luck, Foxx may have broken the mark.

For instance, he hit five shots into a right-field screen at St. Louis. They went as doubles. In Babe's day the screen was not there and Foxx's hits would have been homers. He also hit a newly installed screen at Cleveland three times. Had those two screens not been there, Foxx would have had 66 home runs in 1932. Perhaps, people began to say, the Babe's mark isn't meant to be broken. Foxx had a great ca-

Hank Greenberg (*Detroit Tigers*)

reer and wound up with 534 homers, second best to Babe until the modern sluggers came along.

The next challenge came in 1938. Big Hank Greenberg of Detroit was the challenger. Greenberg had 40 homers and 183 RBIs the year before, so he was ready. In 1938 he was in a groove. In fact, even when he slumped, he was hitting homers.

"There were some points that year," recalled Hank, "that I could hit homers, but not much else. I remember one nine-game stretch when I had just five hits, but all of them were home runs."

Greenberg made a big run at the record. He was in a good position in early September, when he was over fifty. Hank set a record that year by hitting two homers in a game eleven times. With five games left in the season, he had already tied Foxx with 58 home runs.

"I think I can beat the Babe," said Hank.

But in the first game a wild left-hander walked Hank four times. The next game he was up against Bobo Newsom, a pitcher he never hit well. Hank managed just a single. Then the team traveled to Cleveland for the last three games of the year. The first game Hank went hitless. So it all came down to a final Sunday doubleheader.

It was a dark, dismal rainy Sunday when the Indians and Tigers took to the field. Young Bob Feller and his blazing fastball faced the Tigers in the first game. In the darkness of Cleveland's stadium Feller's fastball was untouchable. He set a record by striking out eighteen batters, including Hank twice. In the second game Hank had two doubles, but the umpires then had to call the game in the sixth inning when the rain became too hard.

Mickey Mantle (*New York Yankees*)

"I'm sorry, Hank," the ump said. "But this is as far as I can go."

Hank was a good sport, but saddened, he answered, "That's all right. This is as far as I can go, too."

Ruth's record remained intact once more. For the next twenty-three years no slugger made a serious run at the Ruth record. There were some who threatened in the first half, but August and September always seemed to shut them off. Then came the 1961 season, and fittingly, it was two Yankees who made it look like a rerun of Ruth and Gehrig.

They were Mickey Mantle and Roger Maris. Mantle, of course, was the big favorite. He was a career Yankee, who followed in the Ruth-Gehrig-DiMaggio tradition as the big, slugging superstar. He had already had a 52-homer year in 1956 when he won the triple crown. Like the Babe, Mantle often hit high, long, towering home runs. If anyone should break the Babe's mark, Mantle seemed like the player most destined.

Maris was a different story. He had started his career in Cleveland, then moved on to Kansas City before coming to the Yanks. He was a fine ball player for several seasons, yet many Yankee traditionalists considered him an outsider, a nomad who didn't really belong. He was not born and bred to be a Yankee.

In addition, Maris didn't hit the big, long shots that characterized Ruth and Mantle. He was a line drive hitter who got the knack of pulling the ball into the short right-field stands at Yankee Stadium. Many of his homers there would be long outs or at best extra-base hits in other ball parks, whereas Mantle's homers would be homers in the Grand Canyon.

To make matters worse, Maris was somewhat of an introvert who had difficulty handling the aggressive New York press corps. He often appeared surly and uncooperative. All this added up to make Mantle the big favorite when the two ball players began clouting home runs at a record-breaking clip in 1961.

The Yanks had another powerhouse team that year. They mowed down the opposition with the likes of Yogi Berra, Bill Skowron, Elston Howard, John Blanchard, Hector Lopez, Bobby Richardson, and Tony Kubek. By midseason all eyes were on Mantle and Maris, the M Boys, as one writer dubbed them. Both kept clouting homers at an almost identical pace. Would one of them crack the Babe's mark?

Everyone knew the Mantle story, his background and his rise to the Yanks the same year the great DiMaggio retired. It was like a royal succession. But what about Maris? Born in 1934 in Fargo, North Dakota, Roger was an outstanding high school football star whom many colleges pursued. But he was also a fine baseball player and decided to pass up college and football to sign with the Cleveland Indians.

He started in the minors in 1953 and in 1957 came up to the Indians. The next year he was traded to Kansas City. Maris showed good power then, but nothing outstanding, although he was often slowed by a succession of minor injuries. He was an outstanding right fielder with good range, sure hands, and a powerful arm. He never received full credit for the fine defensive player that he was.

The Yanks were looking to strengthen their outfield in 1960 and made a deal with K.C. for Maris. He promptly responded by making his first Yankee year an outstanding one. He belted out 39 homers and won the league's Most Valuable Player award.

Mantle and the rest of the Yanks commanded most of the

Roger Maris (*New York Yankees*)

headlines at the beginning of 1961. Maris was slumping, with just four homers in his first 29 games. He began to hear the boo-birds at Yankee Stadium, and the critics started calling him a one-year wonder. There was even talk of his being benched for one of the Yanks' high-powered second-stringers.

But suddenly Maris found the groove. He began pulling homers into the right-field seats at the Stadium and hitting them on the road, too. By the end of May he had taken over the league lead in homers, with Mantle right on his heels. The two sluggers kept moving out, leaving the league's other sluggers behind. When Maris reached the 40-homer mark in late July, with Mantle just a few behind, the talk of a new record started anew.

It wasn't easy for Maris. When Mantle would come up at the Stadium, the cheers would rock the old ball park in the Bronx. But when Rog took his place at the plate, there were more boos than cheers. He was the villain. No one wanted him to break that record. All this bothered Maris greatly. He told reporters,

"I never wanted all this fuss. I just wanted to be a good ball player, help my team win ball games, and hit maybe 25 or 30 homers with around 100 RBIs and a .280 average. I just wanted to be one of the guys, an average guy having a good season."

There was no way Roger Maris could be an average guy in 1961. As the homers increased, reporters everywhere surrounded the two sluggers. Mantle could get by with his boyish grin and Oklahoma drawl. But Maris had an increasingly difficult time. Then some baseball people began complaining about the new schedule, with 162 games as compared to 154 in Ruth's day. If either Maris or Mantle broke the mark in the eight extra games, would it count? Baseball Commissioner Ford Frick ruled that if the record were broken after the 154 games were played, it would be so noted in the record book. This made some people angry, including former slugger Hank Greenberg.

"I don't like the idea of people trying to belittle the record before it's even set. As much as I admired the Babe, I feel that he wasn't subjected to the strains of day-and-night baseball, the constant travel, and all the media commotion that must be upsetting to Roger and Mickey. I feel that the accomplishment of breaking the record is greater now than it ever was."

Mantle and Maris both reached the 54-homer mark at about the same time. But Mickey fell victim to a knee injury (injuries plagued his entire career). He was forced from the lineup and virtually eliminated from the race. In fact, he finished with those 54 homers.

Now the pressure was really on Maris. He was alone, and many people were against him. He was having an even harder time with the press, and his nerves were so bad that his hair actually began falling out. Yet that smooth, uppercut swing of his was still in the groove, and he continued to hit home runs.

By the time the Yanks had played 154 games, Maris had 59 homers. He knew then that in the eyes of many he'd never break the record. But he didn't quit. In the 158th game he belted number 60 off Jack Fisher of Baltimore. He now had four games left to try for number 61.

For three games Maris couldn't get his pitch. Now it was the last game of the year, just as it was for the Babe thirty-four years earlier. The Yanks were playing the Red Sox at the Stadium, and the Sox had young Tracy Stallard on the mound. Stallard could have easily pitched around Maris, given him nothing to hit. But instead he took up the challenge and gave it his best. In the first inning he got Rog on a short fly to left.

Then Maris came up again in the fourth. Stallard threw two fastballs, both outside. Figuring Maris would be looking for the curve, Stallard threw his fastball again. This time Rog was ready. He whipped the bat around and the ball headed toward the right-field stands. It was up—and in. He had done it, his 61st home run, and characteristically it gave the Yanks a 1-0 victory.

"I'm glad it's over," Maris said after the game. "I appreciate the fact that Stallard was man enough to pitch to me and give me a chance to hit one."

Roger Maris was baseball's new single-season home run king. Or was he? To many, the Babe was still the King. For some strange reason, his 60 homers were still the standard. Maris was the league's MVP again in '61 and had a pretty good year in 1962. But after that it was downhill. Once again minor injuries slowed him down. He never felt comfortable as a Yankee, maybe because the official "family" never accepted him. He was finally traded to the St. Louis Cardinals, where he found happiness as the good ball player he wanted to be. He was part of Cardinal pennant winners in 1967 and 1968 and closed out his career on a high note.

Strangely enough, Roger Maris never returned to Yankee Stadium and has never come back for one of the Yanks' patented Old Timers' Days. Just a few short years after breaking one of the most famous of all baseball records, Roger Maris was a largely forgotten figure.

Willie Mays (left) and Hank Aaron

There's no way Henry Aaron will ever be a forgotten figure. Even if Hammarin' Hank hadn't hit more career homers than anyone, he'd still be remembered as one of the finest ball players of all time.

Aaron did things smoothly and easily. But he could do everything. He hit for average; he hit with power. He ran exceptionally well and knew how to steal bases. He played the outfield with an effortless grace and had a powerful throwing arm. He was a team player who never worried about personal statistics. To many he was a colorless player, and for that reason it took him a long time to get the recognition he deserved.

Aaron spent the first half of his long career in the shadow of players like Willie Mays, Mickey Mantle, and Roberto Clemente. They were more flamboyant; they made headlines; they created controversy. Aaron just played ball, and year after year he was up among the leaders in average, homers, and runs batted in.

The man they sometimes call Bad Henry was born on February 5, 1934, in Mobile, Alabama. He was one of seven children and spent a childhood pretty much steeped in poverty. He was a loner as a boy, spending countless hours by himself in his backyard. His mother once gave him a top to spin back there, but when she looked out, he was hitting the top with a baseball bat.

As a youngster, Henry saw several major league teams come through Mobile as they barnstormed their way north. After seeing the Yankees come through town one day he went home and announced:

"I'm gonna play baseball just like Joe DiMaggio when I grow up."

Henry was still too young to know that blacks weren't in

the major leagues then, but after World War II he went to the same field and saw Jackie Robinson playing as a member of the Brooklyn Dodgers. That sent his hopes soaring, and Henry became one of a number of southern black youngsters who began harboring dreams of a major league career.

There was no coaching for a youngster like Henry, and when he first started playing ball he batted with his hands crossed. Once he got that straightened out he began hanging line drives all over the lot. His first pro team was the Indianapolis Clowns, one of the top teams in the old Negro Leagues.

That was a rough life. The teams crisscrossed the country in old buses, often wondering where they'd eat and sleep. They often played on fields that resembled cow pastures, and they were paid little for their efforts. There were many legendary black ball players in the Negro Leagues who never got a chance to play in the majors. Only today are they beginning to get some belated recognition.

Luckily for Henry and the blacks who followed, baseball's color line was broken by Jackie Robinson in 1947. After Henry proved an outstanding player with the Clowns, he was signed into the Boston Braves organization and sent to Eau Claire, Wisconsin, in 1952. The next year he was at Jacksonville in the South Atlantic, or Sally League. He was one of three blacks to break the color line in that league. He ran into his share of prejudice, but let his bat talk back with a .362 average, 22 homers, and 125 RBIs. His manager there, Ben Geraghty, remembers:

"Henry was the most relaxed kid I've ever seen," said Geraghty. "Nothing bothered him. During the long bus rides he'd always fall asleep. He could sleep anywhere."

But Henry didn't sleep on the field. He was outstanding

Hank Aaron (*Atlanta Braves*)

there. By 1954 he was with the parent club. Only the Braves were no longer in Boston. The team had moved to Milwaukee, and that's where Hank began his big league career. He got a starting job in spring training when veteran Bobby Thomson was injured and played regularly until he broke his own ankle in early September. It was the only serious injury of his career.

Henry hit .280 that first year, with 13 homers and 69 RBIs. It was a modest start. The next year he became a .300 hitter for the first time and blasted 27 homers and 106 RBIs. Two years after that, in 1958, he was leading the Braves to a pennant with a .322 average, 44 home runs, and 132 RBIs.

There was no doubt that Henry was now one of the finer ball players in the majors. Yet he didn't get the press coverage of a Mays or Mantle. One reason was that they played in New York where the press coverage was better. They had also come up a few years earlier and already had reputations as big blasters. Mickey hit those unbelievably long homers, and Willie ranged all over the outfield, making his patented basket catches.

Aaron, on the other hand, played it cool and easy. He never seemed to exert himself, but he always got the job done. His way proved the best in the long run, since he knew how to pace himself and his body didn't betray him when he reached his late thirties. During one spring training, Hank, as many now called him, ambled into the batting cage, took three swings, then drawled, "Well, ole Hank is ready for another year."

To those who didn't know it would seem as if they were watching a lazy ball player. Well, "ole Hank" was all of twenty-two years old when he made that remark. It was just his way. As the 1950s turned into the 60s, Hank became a model of consistency. While the likes of Mantle, Mays, and even Henry's teammate, Eddie Mathews, outdistanced Aaron in total homers in those days, he slowly gained on them as the others lost time to injury and advancing age.

Looking at Henry's home run totals beginning with his 44 in 1957, his stats run like this—44, 30, 39, 40, 34, 45, 44, 24, 32, 44, 39, 29, 44, 38, 47, 34, 40. Meaningless numbers, perhaps. But this takes Aaron up to 1973, and by then he was making headlines. For he finished the 1973 season just one home run behind Babe Ruth, with 713. He had already knocked in more runs than any other player in history. He was over 3,500 base hits and had a lifetime average of .311. By then everyone recognized him as one of the greatest ever.

Henry's consistency can be seen another way. He hit home run number 200 on July 3, 1960, smashed number 300 on April 19, 1963, hammered number 400 on April 20, 1966, gathered his 500th on July 14, 1968. When he belted number 600 on April 27, 1971, everyone realized he was a threat to break Babe's legendary 714. He was already thirty-seven years old, but he wasn't slowing down. In fact, he finished that 1971 season with 47 round trippers, his best total ever.

Mantle had already retired with 536 homers, Mathews with 511. Mays was still ahead of Henry, but faltering badly. In May 1972 Henry belted number 648 to tie him with Mays. Then he was past Willie and moving towards the Babe.

Some writers tried to compare Henry's chase with that of Roger Maris. But Hank wouldn't take the bait. He looked at it very logically and sensibly.

"There was a different kind of pressure on Roger," he said. "He was under a strict time limit. He had to do it before the season ended or there'd never be another chance. In a way,

I've got all the time in the world. If I don't do it this season, I'll do it next season. In other words, unless I get hit by a truck, I'll do it."

Henry surprised everyone in 1973 with his great 40 home run year at age thirty-nine. There was real drama at the end as he pulled up just short with 713 clouts. But there was another phenomenon that had started with the hoopla, a shameful one that shouldn't happen but always does. Hank began getting a great deal of hate mail, much of it from people who didn't want to see a black man break Babe Ruth's record. This hurt Hank.

"Most of the mail is racial," Henry admitted to the press. "They call me 'nigger' and every other bad word you can imagine. If I was white, all America would be proud of me. As far as I'm concerned, it indicates something very low in this country."

The publicity about the hate mail brought in a new flood of mail supporting the aging slugger, and this made Henry feel better. Still, he was more vocal now than he had ever been in his career.

"People pay to get into the park and are entitled to boo and jeer. But I won't take the racial stuff. I don't have to. I'll tell you one thing. All this is just making me more determined to break the record."

Hank started 1974 needing just one homer to tie. He wasted little time. His first at bat saw him facing Jack Billingham of Cincinnati. After taking two pitches for balls, Henry took his first cut of 1974. He connected, sending a long, high drive to left. Outfielder Pete Rose just watched the ball go out of sight. Henry had hit number 714.

Henry sat out the second game of the year and didn't hit one in the third. Then the team came home. The Braves were now located in Atlanta; they had come from Milwaukee several years before. A huge crowd sat on the edge of their seats as the forty-year-old Aaron came up against Al Downing of the Dodgers.

It took only one swing for Hank to do it. The shot rocketed out of the park and Henry Aaron was baseball's new home run king!

"Thank God it's over," said Henry afterward. He could now get out of the ever-present spotlight, the many questions he had heard over and over again would be no more. The hoopla would die down.

In that sense, Henry was more like Maris than Ruth. He finished the 1974 season with 20 homers, then played two more years for the American League's Milwaukee Brewers, ending his career in 1976 with 755 home runs. He then returned to the Braves as a club executive. Henry will undoubtedly slip from the spotlight. Unlike the Babe, he doesn't need the noise and adulation around him. In fact, he once told a writer:

"I don't want to be anything or anyone special. I just want to be remembered as plain Henry Aaron."

He'll be remembered for much more than that. He set a host of records and was perhaps the finest all-around player of his generation. The thing that he'll be remembered most for is the home run mark, just like Roger Maris before him and the man who started it all before that, Babe Ruth. For to many, the home run is still what the game of baseball is all about.

CHAPTER 5

The Flamethrowers— Baseball's Strikeout Kings

The strikeout artist is to pitching what the home run slugger is to hitting. The pitcher who can fire that ball faster than the rest is looked upon with the same kind of awe as the batter who can hit the ball farther than the rest. Like the home run hitter, the strikeout artist is the one who brings in the crowds and evokes the loudest cheers.

There have been a good number of flamethrowing strikeout pitchers in the history of the national pastime. Lest someone feel slighted, remember the names of Rube Waddell, Lefty Grove, Bob Feller, and Tom Seaver. They're all from different generations and all could fire the pill and get the big whiff. Plus they were outstanding winning pitchers. All of them held or presently hold one or more strikeout marks.

Yet when you talk strikeout, three names seem to jump to the head of the class. They are Walter Johnson, Sandy Koufax, and Nolan Ryan.

Johnson pitched in the early days, in baseball's infancy,

yet the old-timers still insist that he was the fastest. Koufax had his heyday in the 1960s, enjoying five seasons during which he was so overpowering that many called him the best ever. Then he was forced into premature retirement because of a physical ailment. Ryan is the fastballer of the 1970s, a dynamic strikeout artist who has also had to struggle with wildness during his career. But when it comes to pure strikeouts, he may be the best of all time.

The careers of all three men were vastly different in some respects, as were the eras in which they pitched. But when each was on the beam on a good day, his fastball was nearly untouchable, his game just about perfect.

Walter Johnson was known as the Big Train. The nickname right there gives a clue to his strong point. He threw the express, the fastball, and he threw it almost exclusively. In today's game, and it's really been this way for years, if a pitcher came to the majors and had a fastball but nothing else, no curve, no slider, no change-up, the consensus would be that he didn't have a chance to make it. They'd probably send him back to the minors to develop another pitch.

Yet Walter Johnson came up with a fastball and stayed in the majors with a fastball for more than twenty-three years. It wasn't until the waning years of his career that he developed something of a curve. For all those peak years he just threw the fast one. The hitters knew it was coming, but there was very little they could do about it.

There are all kinds of stories about Johnson's speed. Perhaps some of them are legends now, part of baseball's lore. But there are still old timers who swear they are true.

For example, during Johnson's prime he was pitching for his one and only team, the Washington Senators, in a twilight game. Darkness was fast approaching (there were no lights in those days) and the Train had two strikes on the hitter. His catcher, Gabby Street, called time and went to the mound. He and Johnson decided to have some fun. Walter got set, cranked up, and fired—only he didn't release the ball. He held onto it. A split second later catcher Street slammed his bare fist into his mitt.

"Strike three, you're out!" hollered the plate umpire.

The batter just shook his head and walked away. Well, they say that one's true. Walter's speed was so great that in the twilight neither the batter nor umpire was surprised at not even seeing the ball. They just took it for granted that the ball blazed over the plate.

There was another similar incident, in a twilight game, when a hitter came to the plate and before Johnson could deliver, the man struck a match and held it up.

"Hey, what gives?" asked the umpire. "Think that's gonna make you see the ball better?"

"No," replied the hitter, quite seriously. "I'm not worried about that. I just want to be sure Johnson sees me!"

Walter's fastball was a thing to fear. In fact, it sometimes scared the Big Train himself. As he once said:

"I'm really frightened of this thing sometimes. I'm afraid that if I hit someone with it I'll kill him."

That was Johnson. He was as kind and gentle as he was fast. Had Walter been a mean man, willing to brush the hitters back, the ball players may have well refused to hit against him. In fact, the great Ty Cobb went so far as to use Johnson's kindness against him. The Georgia Peach had as much trouble as anyone hitting Walter until one day when he saw the Train accidentally hit one of his teammates. Cobb saw Johnson turn pale with fear until the man got to his feet.

After that Ty would always crowd the plate, banking on Johnson not pitching him tight. Sure enough, Walter always tried to work the outside corner on Ty, and when he got behind on the count, he had to come down the middle. So Ty was ready and wound up with a .300 lifetime average against Johnson. But there weren't many other players with Ty's bravado or batting skills, so that really wasn't the key.

There was no key. Walter spent his entire career pitching for a team that was usually in the second division. You know what they always said about Washington. It went like this. "First in peace; first in war; and last in the American League."

That was often the case. Yet pitching for the Senators from 1907 to 1927, Walter Johnson won 416 games. Only one pitcher ever won more, and that was Cy Young, who started his career before the turn of the century. Johnson, by the way, lost 279, and there are those who say that if Walter pitched for a stronger team, his record would have been by far the most impressive in baseball history.

As it was, the Train won 20 or more games in 12 different seasons. He fanned more than 300 hitters twice and wound up with a total of 3,508 strikeouts, more than any other pitcher in history. He also led the league in strikeouts on 12 occasions. In addition, he is the only pitcher in baseball history to post more than 100 shutouts in his career, finishing with 113, some 23 more than his nearest rival.

One veteran reporter, who followed much of the Johnson career, had an explanation for all the shutouts.

"Walter had to pitch shutouts," the reporter said. "Playing with Washington, that was the only way he could be sure of a win."

Johnson came up when baseball was in its infancy. It was

considered a rough and tumble occupation in those days. Salaries were nowhere near what they are today, though the stars in that era made a comfortable living, even if they didn't emerge as rich men.

In a sense, it was surprising that someone with Walter's background would become a baseball star. There was no radio or television to bring the game to the far reaches of the country, and no teams further west than St. Louis.

Walter Perry Johnson was born in Humboldt, Kansas, on November 6, 1887. His parents, Frank and Minnie Johnson, were farmers who had come from Pennsylvania. Times were tough then and the Johnsons decided to look for a new life. In 1901 they and other poor farmers like them moved to California, where there were all kinds of stories of people becoming rich in the oil business.

Of course, it didn't turn out that way, but the Johnsons were resourceful people. They couldn't get into the oil business, so instead they began supplying the oil people with horses and mules needed for the work. In time, they built up a good business.

Being part of the business helped young Walter to build up massive shoulders and arms, which, in turn, enabled him to throw a ball like a bullet. Soon he was playing baseball with his friends. He started out as a catcher because he threw so hard that there wasn't a catcher around who could handle him. He was the star of the local team, the Oil Field Juniors, when he was about thirteen.

He became a pro in 1906 and was pitching for the Weiser Telephone Company team, which was located in Idaho. At the same time he dug post holes for them. A traveling salesman saw his fastball, and being a friend of Washington manager Joe Cantillon, the man quickly relayed what he

Walter Johnson (*Baseball Hall of Fame*)

saw. Cantillon sent an injured player out to look at Walter and the man immediately handed the twenty-year-old a $100 bill and offered him $350 a month for the rest of the year if he'd join the Senators right away.

Walter agreed and within a short time he was starting his first major league game. It resulted in a 3-2 loss, the first of many low-scoring games he would lose because of Washington's lack of hitting. But he was in the big time now and there to stay.

It took a couple of years for 6-1, 200-pound Johnson to find the groove. He had very little batting support. He was 5-9 his first year, 14-14 in 1908, and a dismal 13-25 the year after that. They didn't keep earned run stats back then, so it's hard to tell how effective Walter was during that 1909 season. One thing is for sure: he already had the fast one as veteran pitcher Nick Altrock remembers.

"Walter was pitching against Detroit one day in 1909," said Altrock, "and the Tigers loaded the bases on a couple of errors and a walk. Now they had their three great left-handed hitters coming up—Ty Cobb, Sam Crawford, and Bobby Veach. You know what ol' Walter did. He struck 'em out on nine pitches, that's what."

The next year, 1910, Walter turned it around. He won 25 and lost 17, beginning a string of ten straight 20-game years. He also struck out 313 batters that year, leading the league in that department for the first time.

He had his greatest season in 1913. That year the Big Train had a record of 36-7, with 12 shutouts, 243 strikeouts, and only 38 walks. It was also the first season that they kept earned run averages in the American League and Walter led everyone with a fantastic 1.14 ERA.

In fact, during the next three seasons his record was 28-18,

27-13, and 25-20. During those seasons his ERAs read 1.72, 1.55, and 1.89. That shows the kind of luck he was pitching in and the kind of hitting support he had. To lose 20 games with an ERA under two runs a game sounds impossible.

Yet Walter never complained, never had a bad word for anyone. He kept pitching, kept clicking off wins, shutouts, and strikeouts. In six of the first seven years they kept earned run averages, Walter was under 2.00.

Johnson was a sidearmer, sweeping the ball across the front of his body. He liked to pitch from a low mound, and since there were no regulations on the fields then, the Senators obliged. As old-time Yankee hurler Waite Hoyt once said, "They kept the mound so flat for him at Washington that pitching in Griffith Stadium was like hurling out of a hole."

In 1920, the mighty Johnson arm showed vulnerability for the first time. It was sore most of the year and Walter slipped to an 8-10 mark. Three more subpar seasons followed. It looked as if he might be washed up. Ironically enough, Washington finally had a pennant contender, and in 1924 they made it to the top.

Walter also turned back the clock, compiling a 23-7 record and leading the league in strikeouts for the twelfth and last time. There was a great deal of sentiment for Walter when the Senators faced the New York Giants in the World Series. Most everybody wanted to see the great veteran win in the Series.

It was tough. Walter lost the opener, 4-3, then was hit hard in the fifth game, losing 6-2. But the Series went to seven, and when the score was tied in the eighth inning, manager Bucky Harris called on the Train.

This time Walter had it. He kept firing his fast one past

the Giant hitters. For four innings he mowed them down until the Senators finally pushed across a run in the last of the twelfth. They had won the World Series and Walter Johnson was the winning pitcher.

It was more of the same the next season. Walter was almost thirty-eight years old, but he had a 20-7 record for the year. This time the Senators faced the Pittsburgh Pirates. Walter started the opener and won it, 4-1, striking out ten Pirates in the process. Four days later he started again, this time shutting out Pittsburgh, 4-0, on six hits. He was looking like the old Train, all right.

The Pirates fought back to tie the Series and send it into a seventh game. Manager Harris decided once more to pitch his aging star. So Walter trudged back to the mound on a cold, rainy day in Pittsburgh to try once more. This time he couldn't do it. He kept slipping on the wet mound and he was tired.

The Pirates got three in the third, though the Senators fought back for a 6-3 lead. But a run in the fifth, another pair in the seventh, and then three big ones in the last of the eighth decided the matter. Pittsburgh won it 9-7, and Walter had stayed in there all the way.

Many people criticized manager Harris for staying with Walter for so long in a crucial game. They felt perhaps a fresh pitcher could have held the Pirates. But Harris wouldn't make excuses.

"There's no man in this world I'd rather have on the mound than Walter Johnson. I don't care how old he is. When you're in a big game, you go with your best, and Walter's the best there is."

It was quite a tribute to the veteran, and, in effect, his last hurrah. He faded to a 15-16 mark the next year, and in 1927 suffered a broken leg that all but finished him. Yet his records are still there, and so are the words of so many who remember him.

Asked to name his most embarrassing moment in baseball, Ty Cobb, the wily one, answered quickly:

"Facing Walter Johnson on any dark day in Washington."

Then there was the time Cleveland shortstop Ray Chapman took two strikes from Johnson and suddenly walked away from the plate.

"Hold it," shouted the umpire. "That's only two strikes."

"I know," answered Chapman. "You can have the third one. It won't do me any good."

Johnson's longtime catcher, Gabby Street, once made headlines of his own by catching a ball dropped from the top of the very high Washington Monument. Reporters gathered around, telling Street what a great accomplishment he had just made. The old catcher laughed.

"Heck, it was easy," he said. "You guys forget that I've been catching Walter Johnson's fastball for years."

Walter Johnson retired to a farm in Maryland, where he raised cattle and hunted with his many dogs. The big guy always loved animals. He did that until he died in 1946, victim of a brain tumor. Even though he was gone, Walter Johnson left behind a legion of records and legends. He was the Big Train, the first and possibly the fastest of baseball's flamethrowers.

Sandy Koufax never had a nickname. He was never called by any name that referred to his blazing fastball or sharp-breaking curve. He was just plain Sandy. For a few years during the 1960s, just plain Sandy was as good a pitcher as there ever was.

Yet Sandy Koufax didn't have an easy career. As a fastballing youngster he was wild and unpredictable. He couldn't find the groove. For a while it looked as if he wouldn't make it as a major league pitcher. Once he found the groove he was unbeatable. Then the injuries started, the first being a circulatory ailment that threatened to end his career. After that it was arthritis in his pitching elbow, which became progressively worse. Koufax pitched the final two years of his career in almost constant, terrible pain. Yet he was still the best pitcher in baseball until the thought of crippling himself for life made retirement completely necessary.

During his time, Sandy teamed with Don Drysdale to give the Los Angeles Dodgers the best one-two pitching combo in the game. Drysdale was a huge 6-6, so Sandy often looked small when the two of them posed together. In reality, Sandy was a powerful 6-2, weighing in the area of 200 pounds. He was even stronger than he looked. His manager, Walter Alston, remembers Sandy from early in his career.

"I took a close look at Sandy one spring," said Alston, "and it looked like he had a roll around his middle. I thought to myself that here was this young pitcher getting fat already. So I grabbed the bulging area to tell him to lose it and I actually pulled my hand back in surprise. It wasn't fat, but a bulge of muscle, rock-hard solid muscle."

The Dodger trainer at the time, Wayne Anderson, also testified to the strength in the Koufax body.

"Sandy had a stronger back than either Ted Kluszewski or Frank Howard," said the trainer, "and they were both huge men. I remember how rough a job it was getting those muscles loose before a game. I had to massage them and then use liniment. And Sandy still had to do all kinds of stretching and bending during the early innings to get loose."

The tightness in his muscular frame was one of Sandy's early problems. He could throw the ball like a bullet, but when he started to get wild, he'd try to throw even harder, and then his back would begin to tighten. Until he discovered the secret of relaxing on the mound, Sandy Koufax would never be a consistently successful pitcher.

Sandy was born on December 30, 1935, in Brooklyn, New York. As a youth, he was drawn more toward education than sports, since that was emphasized in his home. Sandy was a good student who didn't even take his books home in high school and still got good grades.

Soon he was playing ball. Basketball was his first love, as it is for many city kids, but pretty soon he was playing baseball on the sandlots as well. Sandy's friends remember that he always had that strong left arm, and at the same time had very little luck controlling it. Sandy didn't really care then. Basketball was still his first love.

By early 1953, a Brooklyn Dodger scout was tipped off about Sandy and his powerful left arm. The youngster was given a tryout at old Ebbets Field, where he showed he could throw fast, but little else. Then he packed off to the University of Cincinnati on a basketball scholarship. That's how good he was on the court.

Sandy didn't even plan on playing college baseball until he learned the school team was planning a big southern trip. That sounded good to him, so he went out for the team and made it. His first real experience as a pitcher resulted in 52 strikeouts in just 32 innings. He couldn't really control his fastball, but it moved so quickly that people couldn't believe it.

That summer Sandy had a tryout with the Giants. They gave up, figuring he was too wild. But not the Dodgers.

They still wanted him and offered him a bonus of $14,000 and a $6,000 salary. In December 1954, Sandy took the money and signed.

Now the struggle began. Sandy was so nervous that first spring that the powerful muscles tightened up and he couldn't pitch. When he finally worked that out, he was wild. The ball shot in every direction. The Dodger hitters were afraid to face him even in batting practice or intra-squad games. One veteran said:

"Taking batting practice against that kid is like playing Russian roulette with five bullets. You just don't have much of a chance."

Sandy didn't pitch much his rookie year of 1955. He got into just 12 games, had a 2-2 record, struck out 30 in 42 innings, and walked 28. He had really proved nothing, except that he could stick. He was still on the team when 1956 began. Things were about the same that year (a 2-4 mark) and in 1957, when he was 5-4. But that year he struck out 122 hitters in 104 innings and gave a hint of things to come. The next year, the Dodgers moved from Brooklyn to Los Angeles and Sandy went with them.

Sandy got more of a chance the next three years, but he was still mediocre, with records of 11-11, 8-6, and 8-13. Those last two seasons he had 173 and 197 strikeouts. But how long could the Dodgers wait for him to be a winner?

Perhaps the Dodgers would have released or traded him, except that every once in a while Sandy would remind them of his great potential. In 1959 he tied an all-time record (at that time) by striking out eighteen Giants in one game. When L.A. made it to the World Series that year, Sandy got a start and responded by pitching a brilliant game, which he unfortunately lost, 1-0. Then came the disappointing 8-13 mark in 1960. After six years in the majors his record was 36-40. Sandy was so discouraged that he told himself that 1961 would be a make or break year. If he didn't do better, he'd quit the game.

That spring he was having his usual troubles, inconsistency and wildness. Then one day, in a B squad game, a young catcher named Norm Sherry went out to talk with Sandy.

"Hey, let's have some fun out there today," Sherry said. "Don't try to throw that fastball of yours through my glove every time. Ease up a bit, and throw more curves and change-ups."

Sandy decided to try. Suddenly he found he was getting hitters out. By easing up and not throwing as hard, his control improved. His back muscles weren't as tense, and better yet, his fastball had just about the same amount of zip.

When Sandy proved he could do that every time out he was put in the regular rotation, where he promptly won six of his first seven starts.

"If there was a magic formula," he said, "it was pitching every fourth day and knowing I'd stay in the rotation even if I had a bad outing. It was a good feeling."

Sandy finished 1961 with an 18-13 record, leading the league in strikeouts with 269 in just 256 innings. He was no longer just a thrower. He was now a pitcher.

The next year Sandy caught fire. By the end of June he was 10-4 and getting better. Then on June 30, he went up against the New York Mets and came away with the first no-hitter of his career.

"Koufax was untouchable today," wrote one witness. "If the game went eighteen innings the Mets probably wouldn't have gotten a hit. . . . It's hard to say where Sandy has been the past six years, but as of now he looks like the best pitcher to come down the freeway in a long, long time."

By the time Sandy raised his record to 14-4 he looked like a possible 30-game winner. But suddenly he began to lose the feeling in his left index finger. Before long he couldn't grip the baseball. The skin was drying up and scaling off. The ailment was called Reynaud's Phenomenon, in which the blood vessels in the hand constrict and cut off the blood supply. Sandy was out of action. For a while he feared losing his finger.

He came back the last two weeks of the season, only to lose three games. The important thing though was that the finger held up. Sandy was 14-7, with a league-leading 2.54 ERA and 216 strikeouts in just 184 innings. It was still a great year for him and he hoped to stay healthy in 1963.

That was the year Sandy really put it together. He was 25-5, with 306 strikeouts in 311 innings. He led the league again with a 1.88 earned run average, and more important, led the Dodgers into the World Series.

Pitching against the New York Yankees, Koufax was overpowering. He won two games as the Dodgers swept in four. In one, he fanned 15 Yanks to set a record (since broken by Bob Gibson) and wound up with a 1.50 ERA. After it was over he learned that he had been named Most Valuable Player in the National League, as well as winner of the Cy Young Award as best pitcher in the National League. Flame-throwing Sandy had emerged as a superstar.

In 1964 Sandy had the first indication of the arthritis that would end his career. It started early in the year. Sandy explains:

"When you begin to stretch the muscles of the arm in spring training, there are scar tissue and adhesions which do

Sandy Koufax (*Los Angeles Dodgers*)

not stretch but have to be torn away. When this tissue tears, some bleeding and swelling takes place and a pitcher may have to rest for ten days or two weeks. It doesn't happen with every pitcher, but with quite a few."

It happened with Sandy. He missed nearly two weeks, then returned and was once again the best in baseball. By August he was on fire, having won fifteen of his last sixteen starts. But he also hurt his left elbow one day diving into second base. The morning after winning his nineteenth game, Sandy awoke to a strange and frightening thing. He remembers:

"I literally had to drag my left arm out of the bed. It was like a log, a waterlogged log. Where it had been swollen outside the joint before, it was now swollen all the way from the shoulder down to the wrist; inside, outside, everywhere. For an elbow, I had a knee. That's how big it was. And the whole arm was locked in a kind of hooked position. I couldn't straighten it out or bend it. I could actually hear a liquid swishing around in it."

That was enough to frighten anyone. Sandy learned it was traumatic arthritis, a disease that would get progressively worse. Rest would control, but not cure it. When he was hurt Sandy was 19-5 with a 1.74 ERA and 223 strikeouts. He was unquestionably the best in baseball. Now he was finished for the year and his future was once again in doubt.

There was pain right from the start in spring training. That's when the team doctor had a plan. He told Sandy to skip throwing between starts and pitch on game days. The plan worked. Sandy was more dominant than ever.

He won 26 games, lost just eight, and set a new major league record with 382 strikeouts in 336 innings. He once again led the league with a 2.04 ERA and became the first pitcher in baseball history to pitch four no-hitters in his career. The fourth was that baseball rarity, a perfect game. He then won two games in the World Series and had an 0.38 ERA in the fall classic. You couldn't convince the opposition that Sandy was a man in constant pain. After his perfect game, Chicago's great Ernie Banks said:

"He tried to throw the ball right past us, and he did."

Ater taking his second Cy Young Award, Sandy explained how it was.

"Someone said my arm was sore except between the first and ninth innings of the game. I don't blame them for the sarcasm, but it was close to the truth. The act of pitching seemed to pump the fluid out of the elbow joint and through the arm, where it could be more fully absorbed. It actually felt much better when I pitched."

To some, Sandy was at his most brilliant in 1966. He didn't miss a single turn and was again overpowering. His fastball seemed as lively as ever, his curve broke sharply, and he was just thirty years of age. But the pain was worse than ever. He had trouble sleeping after games and had to take many painkillers, which he hated. Baseball was becoming torture for him.

His record was outstanding. It was 27-9, and his 317 strikeouts made him the first man to get more than 300 whiffs in three seasons. His earned run average was his best ever, 1.73, and he won the Cy Young Award for a third time. Many were beginning to call him the most overpowering and best pitcher they'd ever seen.

Several weeks after the season ended, Sandy called a news conference and shocked the baseball world. He was retiring; he wasn't even thirty-one years old.

"I've had a few too many shots and too many pills because

of my arm," he said. "I don't want to take the chance of permanently disabling myself. I have no regrets, not for one minute of my twelve years in baseball. But if I keep on, I could regret one season too many."

Sandy left, after winning 165 games and losing just 87. Those stats don't match up with some of the other greats, but they don't have to. For during his five best years, Sandy Koufax was King of the Hill, the best pitcher alive, and one of the best ever. In fact, five years after he retired, Sandy was voted into baseball's Hall of Fame.

In many ways, the career of Nolan Ryan parallels that of Sandy Koufax. Ryan came up a wild, undisciplined flame-thrower who had to learn how to pitch. He hasn't achieved the overpowering consistency that Sandy did, but when he's right, Ryan is unbeatable, a strikeout pitcher par excellence.

Before talking about Nolan's records, let's go back and see how it happened. Lynn Nolan Ryan was born in Refugio, Texas, on January 31, 1947, and still lives in nearby Alvin. He was the last of six children and got his first experience pitching papers for some spending money. Soon he was into sports.

"I played everything then," he recalls. "But even when another sport became my favorite for a while, I always managed to play a lot of baseball. I was a shortstop at first and didn't begin pitching until high school. Soon after the scouts were coming around. I guess it was because I threw so hard."

Nolan was a skinny 6-2, 150-pounder then, but that arm was live and the New York Mets offered him a $20,000 bonus in 1965. He took it and went to Marion of the Appalachian League, where he fanned 115 batters in just 78 innings. Yet his wildness often got him into trouble and he had a losing record. Playing in the Western League in 1966, he had 272 strikeouts and a 17-2 mark. He looked like a boy wonder, and the Mets called him up for a look at the end of the year.

The next year Nolan was out with a sore arm, but in 1968 he came to the Mets to stay. Many think that was a mistake. A pitcher with control problems must work regularly. With the big club, Nolan was a spot starter and reliever, so his control didn't improve. He was 6-9 that year, with 133 strikeouts in 134 innings. It could have been worse, but could have been a lot better, too.

Then came 1969, the year of the Mets miracle pennant and World Series win. Nolan didn't pitch much that year. He was 6-3 with 92 strikeouts. He made strong relief appearances in the play-offs and World Series, but there was no consistency.

That's how Nolan's Mets career went. The next year he was 7-11 and in 1971 his record was 10-14. He had 116 walks in 152 innings. He was as wild as ever. The Mets just about gave up on the strong-armed righthander. Before the 1972 season they traded him to the California Angels.

Nolan didn't like leaving New York. But he knew he'd get a chance to pitch regularly with the Angels and that was the important thing. Before the season started Nolan talked about some of his problems.

"A fastballer usually has control problems," he said. "There is always a tendency to overthrow, to try to put more on the ball. And the fastballer tends to rely on one pitch because it worked for him when he was young. You can't get away with that in the major leagues."

So Nolan had to do what Sandy Koufax had done before

Nolan Ryan (*California Angels*)

him; he had to cut down on his motion and delivery. He had to get his rhythm. Then Nolan learned something else about flamethrowers.

"Fastballers have to be stronger physically than any other type of pitcher," he said. "That's because they put more into their pitching, from the beginning to the end of each pitch, and the beginning to the end of each game. If the man expects to throw as hard in the ninth as in the first, he's got to be in top condition."

Nolan finally got the chance to pitch regularly, and he made the most of it. Wildness still troubled him, but not as often, and he lost some games because the Angels did not have a good hitting team. When it was over his record was 19-16, with 20 complete games and a fine, 2.28 ERA. He also amazed everyone with 329 strikeouts in just 284 innings. People said he was a threat to Koufax's mark of 382.

"I was conscious of setting up hitters for the first time in 1972," Nolan said. "I was throwing to spots. If I can hit the spots consistently, the strikeouts will come."

The next year he was even better. Pitching every fourth day he became the most feared pitcher in the league. In the space of a month he fired two no-hitters, one against the Royals and another against the Tigers. With just one start left, Nolan had a 20-16 mark and 367 strikeouts. To break Koufax's record, he'd have to strike out sixteen Minnesota Twins. That wouldn't be easy.

Nolan was throwing the hard one, the express, that day. He mowed the Twins down, fanning many of them with his fastball. By the eighth inning he already had 14 strikeouts. Facing Steve Brye, Nolan burned one in on a 2-2 pitch and got him. That strikeout tied the record of 382.

In the ninth he was tired. He still needed one more strikeout, but he didn't get it. Fortunately, the game was tied and went into extra innings. Still, he couldn't get another strikeout in the tenth. Then with two out in the eleventh, the manager came out and asked Nolan how he felt.

"Tired," he said, "but I've got to get one more strikeout."

Facing lefthanded hitter Rich Reese, Nolan reached back for every ounce of strength in his tired body. He fired three straight high inside fastballs. Reese swung at all three and missed. Nolan had done it, and his inspired teammates pushed across a run to give him the win.

What a season! A 21-16 record, 2.87 ERA, and 383 strikeouts in 326 innings. He also fanned 10 or more in 23 different games, another record. He was still a bit wild though, with 162 walks.

The next year Nolan was just as good. He won 22 games, and struck out 367 in 333 innings, becoming the first man to get 300 strikeouts three years in a row. He also tied another mark by striking out 19 in a game. If it wasn't for his occasional wildness, he'd be untouchable.

Nolan started off in 1975 as if he was going to have another great season. In fact, he tossed his third no-hitter early in the year, after which one American League manager said:

"More than any other pitcher I've ever seen, Nolan has the potential to throw a no-hitter whenever he's on the mound."

Unfortunately, it wasn't to be another banner season. Nolan ran into physical problems, arm trouble again. His season was cut short. He wound up with a 14-12 record and 186 strikeouts in 198 innings. He also walked 132 batters. Wildness continued to plague him.

In 1976 he stayed pretty much healthy, but wildness and the continued weak hitting of the Angels hurt him. He did throw his fourth no-hitter, tying the record set by Sandy

Koufax, then said he'd love to pitch a fifth to set the mark before he's through.

Toward the end of the year he picked up and was again pitching overpowering baseball. When it ended he had a 17-18 mark. That isn't really Hall of Fame stuff, but there were some other things to look at. Nolan completed 21 games. Pitchers who complete 20 games or more are usually big winners who had outstanding seasons. He also had a 3.36 earned run average, not as good as the past, but better than many.

Then, of course, there were the strikeouts. He regained the major league lead from teammate Frank Tanana by fanning 327 batters in just 284 innings. He still had the big one going for him, and it broke another of Koufax's records, for it made Nolan the only pitcher to strike out more than 300 batters in four different seasons. The problem was that he walked 183 hitters, giving him nearly 100 more walks than any other pitcher in the league. In 1977 he had more than 300 strikeouts for a fifth time, extending his own amazing record. Wildness continued to cause him to lose some games.

That separates Nolan Ryan from the other big flamethrowers. Both Johnson and Koufax learned to control their fastballs. Nolan has not. As a flamethrower and strikeout artist, he may be the best, but as a pure pitcher, he's still got a ways to go.

No matter what Nolan's record, he continued to bring fans to the ball park, as did Walter Johnson and Sandy Koufax. For there's something about the fastballer, the flamethrower, that makes him stand out from the rest. Perhaps it was best explained by a fellow pitcher, Claude Osteen. Osteen was an effective pitcher in both leagues during the 1960s and early '70s. In fact, he won twenty games on more than one occasion. But he relied on breaking balls, control, changing speeds, all cute stuff. He admired the flamethrowers.

"A great fastball is the finest piece of equipment a pitcher can have," Osteen said. "And I'll tell you why. When a pitcher gets to the seventh or eighth inning of a close game, he's really got to bear down. A pitcher with a great fastball can just take the play away from the hitters. But it takes an exceptional man to do this, one with stamina, concentration, and character. I often saw Koufax do it when I was with the Dodgers.

"He was usually amazing, but on exceptional days he was unreal in the late innings. Around the seventh or eighth he'd get a certain look in his eye and just start blowing the ball past the hitters. He'd challenge everyone. The hitters knew what he was going to throw, but he'd throw it anyway. The ball came in like a blur."

Have things really changed? Is Osteen's statement so different from Ty Cobb's of a half-century earlier when he was asked about his most embarrassing moment? Remember what he said:

"Facing Walter Johnson on any dark day in Washington."

CHAPTER 6

Murderers' Row, the Gas House Gang, the Big Red Machine—A Trio of Superteams

In 1927 they were called Murderers' Row; in 1934 the name was the Gas House Gang; and in 1976 it was the Big Red Machine. During each of the aforementioned years, these teams were the best in baseball and among the greatest of all time. Their appealing nicknames gave them even more of an identity, and the cast of characters that made up these superteams completed the picture.

Without the nicknames they were the New York Yankees, St. Louis Cardinals, and Cincinnati Reds. They were by no means the only great teams in the history of the game. There were many others. But for a combination of reasons, these three were high on the list of the most memorable.

The three teams were not carbon copies of one another. Both Murderers' Row and the Big Red Machine buried the opposition during the season and breezed to pennants. The Gas House Gang had to come from behind to win. Murderers' Row did it with power, the Gas House Gang with speed, the Big Red Machine with a combination of both.

There were more differences. Murderers' Row had a good, but not great pitching staff; the Gas House Gang had a superpitcher who brought others up to his level; the Big Red Machine had a spotty starting staff and very strong bullpen.

Each of the three teams had its league's most valuable player that year, and many records, both team and individual, were set.

Begin with the 1927 Yankees. That was a magic year all around. It was the year the mighty Babe Ruth hit his 60 home runs and Lou Gehrig, second with 47, emerged as a full-fledged star in his own right as American League MVP. The team was also full of other stars, such as Earle Combs, Tony Lazzeri, Bob Meusel, Mark Koenig, Joe Dugan, Herb Pennock, Waite Hoyt, and George Pipgras, to name some of them. They were managed by a colorful, tough little man, Miller Huggins.

The 1934 Cardinals were also colorful, perhaps the most colorful of the three. They had to fight for every inch on the field and often brawled among themselves, as well. They had a playing manager, a Hall of Famer in Frankie Frisch, but he was hard-pressed to control the others, the likes of Joe "Ducky" Medwick, Pepper Martin, and Leo Durocher. The pitching staff was led by none other than Dizzy Dean, one of baseball's greatest characters as well as greatest pitchers. He won thirty games that year, the last National Leaguer to do so, and to make it more complete, had his little brother Paul as a rookie on the team as well.

In 1976 the Cincinnati Reds practically had their own all-star team at the eight regular positions. Their lineup was devastating as the team compiled a .280 average. Six of the top eleven hitters in the league were Redlegs. Their names are well known to today's fans: Rose, Morgan, Bench, Perez, Foster, Griffey, Geronimo, Concepcion. They were truly a powerhouse, with Morgan the league's MVP, Rose leading the N.L. in hits, and Foster leading in RBIs.

The Yankees began building their Murderers' Row team in the early 1920s. The club was purchased by a pair of millionaires, Colonel Jacob Ruppert and Colonel Til Huston. They were determined to make the team into a winner, even if it cost them a good deal of money.

Their best and biggest move came before the 1920 season. That's when they shelled out $125,000 for a lefthanded pitcher, who also played the outfield. His name, of course, was Babe Ruth. Once in New York, Babe became a full-time outfielder and hitter and was the center of the building franchise.

With the Babe beginning to blast all those home runs, the Yanks won pennants in 1921, 1922, and 1923. In each of those World Series they met their crosstown rivals, the New York Giants. The Giants took the first two Series, then the Yanks won their first world championship in 1923. By then the team was already picking up the other players who would star in 1927. Outfielder Bob Meusel was already there, as was third baseman Joe Dugan, and pitchers Waite Hoyt, Bob Shawkey, and Herb Pennock.

In 1924 and 1925 the Washington Senators were American League champs, but the Yanks continued to build. Lou Gehrig became the regular first baseman in 1925 and continued there for 2,130 straight games, a record. During those years the team also added the likes of Combs and Koenig. In 1926 they picked up Tony Lazzeri.

By 1926 the club was ready. Ruth carried the offense with a 47-homer, 155 RBI season. Young Gehrig began showing his stuff. He had 16 homers and 107 RBIs. Of course, no one was aware then that he'd emerge as a real superstar the next season. The Yanks managed another pennant in 1926 and then played a fateful World Series against the St. Louis Cardinals.

It went the full seven games, and in that final contest baseball history was made. With the Cards leading in that game by a 3-2 score in the seventh inning, the Yanks started to rally. Finally, they loaded the bases with two out, and Cardinal manager Rogers Hornsby looked to his bullpen. He then summoned an unlikely pitcher.

He was thirty-nine-year-old Grover Cleveland Alexander, one of the greatest ever, but now in the twilight of his career. Alex the Great had already turned back the clock to win two games for the Cards and didn't expect to pitch again. Legend has it that he had been celebrating the night before and was actually sleeping in the bullpen when the word came to warm up. But he got ready and came in to face young Tony Lazzeri.

Though a rookie, Lazzeri had knocked in more than 100 runs that year. He could hit. Alexander got a strike on Tony, then tried a fastball. Lazzeri smashed a long drive to left. For a minute it looked gone, then suddenly hooked foul. Taking a deep breath, Alexander pulled himself together and fired again. This time Lazzeri swung—and missed! He was out. Alex then retired the Yanks in the eighth and ninth to win the Series for St. Louis.

The Yanks came into the 1927 season with something to

prove. But many people were picking the Athletics to win. Connie Mack was building another powerful team in Philadelphia. As long-time American League umpire Billy Evans said in spring training that year:

"The Athletics are by far the most impressive team I've looked at this spring. They don't seem to have a single weakness."

When the Yanks opened the season with a series against the A's, everyone made a big deal of it. In the first game, Waite Hoyt pitched the Yanks to an 8-3 win. The next day it was the Yanks again, this time getting 16 hits and winning, 10-4. The next game was called because of darkness with the score tied at 9-9, but the following day the Yanks won again, 6-3, behind Herb Pennock. In the opening series, they had already given the A's a solid lesson.

It went on from there. Soon Ruth began hitting home runs, and to everyone's surprise, Gehrig was blasting them out at about the same pace and driving in even more runs than the Babe. With help from Combs, Meusel, and the rest, the team was scoring runs in bunches. They were murdering everyone in sight. Soon the Murderers' Row tag was hung on them.

The next time they met Philly, the A's finally won a game. But the day after, the Yanks showed again why they were to become Murderers' Row. Gehrig and Lazzeri each hit three-run homers and ended with five RBIs. In all, the team blasted out 18 hits and won, 13-6.

Before long the Yanks were making a runaway of the American League race and, in fact, setting a record-breaking pace to do it. Fans were flocking to the new huge ball park in the Bronx, Yankee Stadium, which had opened in 1923. They kept coming long after it was obvious the Yanks would

1927 Yankees, "Murderers' Row". Lou Gehrig is standing to the extreme left in the back row, Babe Ruth is fifth from the left in the back row, and manager Miller Huggins is fifth from the left in the middle row. (*New York Yankees*)

win. They kept coming because Ruth and Gehrig were staging a tight race of their own.

Both sluggers had far outdistanced any competition in the homer race. Everyone knew what Ruth could do. The Babe had already set the mark of 59 some years earlier. But Gehrig only had 16 homers in 1926, and suddenly he was keeping up with the great Bambino. At one point, Gehrig himself admitted he was greatly influenced by Babe and by the homers.

"For a time I tried to change my swing and make it more like Babe's," he said. "But now I'm going back to just meeting the ball."

Babe hit them high and handsome, Lou hung them out to dry, slamming vicious line drives. Yet enough of them reached the seats. It was difficult for the younger man. He knew everyone idolized Babe, and he admitted he'd always be second fiddle when he said:

". . . when Babe's turn at bat is over, whether he strikes out or belts a home run, the fans are still talking about him when I come up. If I stood on my head at the plate, nobody'd pay any attention."

The two sluggers weren't the only ones doing the damage. Combs, Meusel, and Lazzeri were all powerful hitters, and the others were good too. Put together, Murderers' Row just walloped the hide off the ball.

In early July Gehrig slammed his twenty-fourth home run to again tie him with the Babe. More people were talking record, and Babe told a reporter,

"If I am to break my record, I believe I'll do it this year. And there is just one thing that makes me think I can better the 59 mark. That's Lou Gehrig. Having him follow me in the batting order has helped me a lot this year. For most pitchers realize that putting Ruth on to get at Gehrig is the bunk. It's just putting one more run on the path for Lou to drive in."

Around midseason Gehrig was batting at .388, Ruth .356, Combs .336, and Lazzeri .303. In addition several part-time players were hitting well above .300. And the home run race continued. Gehrig blasted his 31st to put him one up on the Babe.

As mid-August approached it was still close. Gehrig actually had a 37-34 lead at one point, yet the Babe was the first to reach 40, leaving Gehrig one behind.

The Yanks maintained a big lead all year. But whenever a team would get hot and look as if it would make a run at them, the Bronx Bombers would take care of it, usually in a head-to-head series. As one Yankee veteran said, years later:

"When we had to win we stuck together and played with a fury and determination that could only come from team spirit. We had a pride in our performance that was very real. It took on the form of snobbery. We felt we were superior people, and I do believe we left a heritage that became a Yankee tradition."

There was a great deal of truth to that. In September the team was closing in on the American League record of 106 wins, Gehrig had a shot at Ruth's RBI mark of 170, and Ruth himself, having finally left Gehrig behind, was chasing his own homer mark.

That's exactly what happened. The club finished with a 110-44 record and the pennant. Gehrig wound up with 47 homers, but his 175 RBIs was a new record, and his .373 batting average helped him win the MVP award. Ruth didn't disappoint anyone either. On the final day of the season he belted number 60 off Tom Zachery of Washington.

The pitchers weren't bad, either. Hoyt had a 22-7 mark. Urban Shocker was 18-6, Wilcy Moore 19-7, and Herb Pennock 19-8. Put it all together and the Yanks won the pennant by 19 games over Philadelphia. Now Murderers' Row would go up against the Pittsburgh Pirates in the World Series. Despite the Yanks' super season, there were people predicting a Pittsburgh victory. Cardinal manager Rogers Hornsby was one. He remembered his club whipping the Yanks the year before.

"The Pirates will out-hustle the Yanks," said the Rajah, "just as all National teams do. That hustling and fighting spirit causes the breaks that mean so much in a short Series like this."

The Babe himself remembered what happened when the Pirate players came out and watched the Yanks take batting practice at Forbes Field before the Series started.

"Most of them had never seen us before, so they stopped and began watching. . . . We really put on a show. Our practice pitcher was just grooving them and Lou and I banged ball after ball into the rightfield stands. I finally blasted one right out of the park in center. Then Bob Meusel and Tony Lazzeri came up and started hammering balls into the leftfield stands the same way. One by one the Pirate players got up and left the park, many of them shaking their heads in disbelief."

That set the stage. In the first game Hoyt and Moore combined to stop the Pirates, 5-4. Then Pipgras won, 6-2. The third game saw Pennock pitch a nifty three-hitter and win, 8-1. Then in the fourth game Moore came back to pitch a 4-3 victory, giving the Yankees a four-game sweep.

Strangely enough, it was the Yankee pitching that won it. Shortstop Koenig was the leading hitter with 9 for 18 and a

.500 average. Ruth hit two homers and batted .400. But Gehrig was worried about his mother who was undergoing surgery and hit "just" .308 on 4-13. He didn't hit any homers, however, and neither did anyone in the series but the Babe.

The team had another fine year in 1928. They won the pennant, but it was close, as the improving A's almost caught them. Then they swept another Series, this time from St. Louis. But it wasn't quite the same as the year before. For the next three years the A's won, before the Yanks regained the title in 1932.

The 1927 team stood out. The majority of baseball people down through the years have continued to regard the club as the greatest ever. When anyone mentions Murderers' Row, they are referring to just one team in one year—the 1927 Yankees.

The St. Louis Cardinals were a powerful National League team in the 1920s and 1930s. They won pennants in 1926, 1928, 1930, 1931, and 1934. Those five pennants brought three World Series triumphs. The Cards had good teams on each of those occasions, but the last team, the 1934 Cards, was something special. They were the outfit that became known as the Gas House Gang.

The Gas House Gang was not like Murderers' Row. They didn't blow the opposition off the field. They just kept sniping at them, one way or the other, until they beat them down. Sure, there were home run sluggers in those days, but the 1934 Cardinals played a different kind of game.

It was a rough game where the players gave no quarter. As one observer said, the game was played largely by farm boys who cared only about one thing—baseball. They played the game as if it were war.

There weren't as many famous names on the Cardinal roster as there had been on the '27 Yanks. But the most memorable ones will never be forgotten.

The playing-manager was Frankie Frisch, the Fordham Flash, a Hall of Fame second baseman who came to the Cards in a trade with the Giants for Rogers Hornsby. Frisch had his hands full that year, trying to cope with the many personalities on his club. There was Joe "Ducky" Medwick, a Hall of Famer who compiled a .324 lifetime average. Medwick was a hitter in every sense of the word. When he wasn't using his bat, he was working with his fists.

Then there was Pepper Martin, nicknamed the Wild Horse of the Osage, because of his derring-do on the basepaths. Martin wasn't the world's greatest hitter, but he could run, and would run, whenever he had the chance. Martin was once described as an above-average ball player who became a superman in the World Series. If the 1931 and 1934 Series are an indication, that was true. Martin would do anything to win, including putting his body on the line, as he belly-flopped all over the field.

Leo Durocher was the team's shortstop. Leo was never a great player, having gained later fame as a manager, but Leo the Lip was a great man to have on a team because he wasn't afraid to say the things that had to be said.

There were other fine players on that Cardinal team, such as first baseman Rip Collins, catcher Bill DeLancy, and pitcher Tex Carleton. Each of these players made his own special contribution to the Gas House Gang. But if you had to pick one man who stood out and typified what this team was all about, it would have to be Jay Hanna Dean, better known to everyone as Dizzy.

Dizzy Dean was a right handed pitcher of the first rank. He

was a fastballer who liked to brag, and more often than not did what he said he'd do. Diz was on the way to a brilliant career, as his 30-7 record of 1934 indicated. But he was hit on the toe by a line drive during the 1937 All-Star Game, tried to come back before the toe was healed, altered his delivery, and hurt his arm. He was never the same again. He was brilliant enough, however, during four peak seasons before the injury to make it into the Hall of Fame.

That wasn't all about Dizzy Dean. He was one of baseball's greatest characters, and never did it show up more than during the 1934 season.

It started right away in spring training when Dizzy's younger brother, Paul Dean, later known as Daffy, was a rookie trying to make the club. Diz let everyone know exactly what he and Paul planned to do that year. He had already signed a contract, but when Paul signed for only about $3,000, Diz fumed.

"You cheated my brother," he yelled at club officials. It was Dizzy who held out, while Paul worked to make the team. It was perhaps the first and only time in baseball history that one player held out because of the contract of another.

Well, Paul finally got about $500 more and Diz suited up. Asked if he would be ready in time, Diz answered,

"Don't worry, my arm is made of rubber. I'll be ready to pitch in two days."

Then someone asked him how many games he and Paul would win that year, and without pausing, Diz answered, "Forty-five."

The reporters laughed. One then asked how many of those Dizzy was going to win.

"Whatever Paul don't win," was the answer.

That was Dizzy Dean for you. He wasn't kidding. Diz always believed everything he said.

It wasn't an easy pennant race for the Cards. In fact, they spent the better part of the season chasing the Giants, who had gotten off fast and stayed on top. Whenever Dizzy faced the Giants, he'd beat them. One observer said it was because Diz once hit seven straight Giant batters in an exhibition game after they had scored seven runs off him. It was only then that the umpire apologetically asked manager Frisch to take Diz out of the game. Even the fun-loving Dean had that meanness in him.

Still, the Cards trailed the Giants, trying to put it all together while battling the opposition and battling each other. In one doubleheader Diz piched a three-hit shutout in the opener. In the second game, brother Paul hurled a no-hitter.

"Heck," said Diz afterward, "if I'da knowed Paul was gonna pitch a no-hitter, I'da pitched one, too." A lot of people believed him.

Finally, it came down to the last weeks. There were sixteen games left and the Cards still trailed the Giants by five and one-half games. The team was winning though, and ball players, being a superstitious breed, didn't want to change their luck. So they didn't even wash their uniforms, despite having played on muddy fields on several occasions. When they arrived in New York they looked like a bunch of Raggedy Andys, covered with mud and grime. Yet they swept a doubleheader from the Jints to close the gap.

The next day a cartoon by Willard Mullin appeared in the New York *World-Telegram*. The cartoon showed two large gas tanks sitting on the wrong side of the railroad tracks. Crossing the tracks were a group of ball players. Instead of carrying bats on their shoulders they were carrying clubs.

1934 Cardinals, "The Gas House Gang". Dizzy Dean is second from right, back row; Leo Durocher, fourth from right, back row; playing manager Frank Frisch, seventh from right, back row; Paul Dean, eighth from right, back row; Pepper Martin fifth from left, back row; and Joe "Ducky" Medwick is standing to the left of the front row, leaning on the bat. (*Baseball Hall of Fame*)

The ball players had the uniform of the St. Louis Cardinals, and under the cartoon it read: *THE GAS HOUSE GANG.* It's not certain whether Mullin got the name somewhere else or made it up, but that's about the time it became well known.

Five days after the doubleheader sweep, the Cards were back in Brooklyn for another twin bill. This was the one in which Diz pitched a three-hitter in the opener, and brother Paul a no-hitter in the nightcap. There were now six games left for the Cards, two in Pittsburgh and four in Cincinnati, and they still trailed the Giants by two games. The Gas House Gang had to scramble.

With the chips down, ol' Diz was pitching with about two days' rest on most occasions. He started by beating Pittsburgh, but the Pirates beat Paul in the second game. Once again Diz assured everyone that "me 'n Paul" will take care of the Reds.

He was just about right. He shut out Cincy in the first game to bring the Cards into a tie with the Giants. Then Paul won, and the Dodgers beat the Giants to put St. Louis into the lead. Before the third game the Cards heard that the Giants had already lost. Naturally, Diz insisted on pitching, since another win would make him a 30-game winner. Sure enough, he pitched another shutout to clinch the pennant for the Cards.

Diz had made good another boast. His 30 wins, plus 19 for Paul, gave the brothers 49 for the season. Everyone had laughed when Dean had predicted they'd win 45. But they weren't the only bright spots for the Cards that year.

Manager Frisch was a .300 hitter once again, as was Medwick, who also cracked 18 triples to lead the league there. Rip Collins was the league home run leader with 35 and also led in slugging percentage and total bases. Pepper Martin was the league's top base thief. Diz, with his 30-7 record, had the best winning percentage and led the league in strikeouts.

Now the Gas House Gang went into the World Series, and it wouldn't be easy. They'd be facing the tough Detroit Tigers, with such all-time greats as Mickey Cochrane, Hank Greenberg, and Charlie Gehringer. But as usual Dizzy Dean assured everyone that things would be all right, that "me 'n Paul" will take care of the Tigers.

Diz opened things up for the Cards with his usual two days' rest. He was also pitching in enemy territory in Detroit. But that didn't bother the tall, slim righthander, who figured whenever he got in a jam he'd call on his great fastball, and, as Diz said, just "fog 'em through."

The Cards didn't waste any time, scoring a pair in the second, one in the third, one in the fifth, then wrapping it up with four in the sixth. Diz wasn't overpowering, but he did the job with an eight-hitter and 8-3 win. Detroit then came back to even things up, 3-2, with Schoolboy Rowe the winner. In the third game the Daffy half of the brother act, Paul, pitched the Cards to a 4-1 victory and 2-1 lead in games.

Game four was all Tigers. Detroit blasted out thirteen hits to take a 10-4 verdict and even the Series once more. That wasn't the highlight of the game, however. What happened could have been a disaster for the Cards. In the fourth inning the game was still close and St. Louis had a man on first. Pinch hitter Spud Davis then singled. Davis was one of the slowest players in the majors. It was assumed there'd be a pinch runner for him.

Before manager Frisch could make a move, a runner came

dashing from the dugout. It was none other than ol' Diz himself. Diz also figured he was as good a baserunner as anyone and had a habit of putting himself in the game to pinch run. This time it almost backfired.

Pepper Martin was up next and hit a bouncer to second, the second baseman picked it up and flipped to the shortstop, who then fired to first to try for the double play. But the ball never got there. Instead, it hit Diz right smack in the forehead. He had forgotten to duck.

Dizzy was out cold and had to be carried from the field. This was pretty serious since he was scheduled to pitch the next day. Fortunately, all he had was a headache and a big lump. Yet some say he wasn't as overpowering as usual the next day and he was beaten by a strong effort by Tommy Bridges, 3-1. Now Detroit had a 3-2 lead with the final pair of games back in Detroit. It looked bleak.

Luckily, there was another Dean in the wings. Paul Dean pitched the sixth game and bested Schoolboy Rowe, 4-3, as the Cards pushed over the winning run in the seventh inning. Now it was down to the seventh game. All the Cardinals fans figured they'd see Dizzy in game seven. But he almost blew it.

This time it was with Frisch, who was going over the hitters before the game. The word is that Diz stood up and told Frisch that going over the hitters was a waste of time because the Tigers weren't going to get any runs off him anyway. Frisch exploded and said he wasn't going to start the star righthander. It took almost to game time for cooler heads to prevail and for the manager to give Diz the OK to warm up.

As for suspense, that was over in the third inning when the Cards combined some timely hits with the Detroit lapses for a seven-run inning. That was all Diz needed. He was so charged up that he wouldn't even sit down in the dugout. He was planning to fully enjoy the rest of the game.

Diz was having no trouble with big Hank Greenberg by pitching him high and tight, the way the scouting reports said to. But with a lead, he decided to challenge Greenberg by pitching high and away. Sure enough, Greenberg singled, but Diz got out of the jam.

Later, when the score was 11-0, Diz called everyone in to ask if they thought he was as good a pitcher as the Giants' Carl Hubbell. Everyone then reassured him. Diz then figured that if he was as good as Hubbell, he could throw a screwball just like Hubbell. He started experimenting right out there in the seventh game of the World Series.

In the sixth inning there was almost a full-scale riot. Joe Medwick tripled, and when he came into third, spikes high, Tiger third baseman Marv Owen tried to stomp him with his own foot. In true Gas House Gang fashion, Medwick came up swinging. When Ducky returned to left field at the end of the inning, the Detroit fans began throwing anything they could get their hands on at him. The game was stopped, and finally Commissioner Kenesaw Mountain Landis ordered that Medwick be removed from the game for his own safety. Fortunately, it was all but over then.

The Cards went on to win, 11-0. Dizzy Dean had once again lived up to his prediction by pitching a shutout and giving up just six hits. To make it even merrier for ol' Diz, both he and Paul had won two games apiece for the Cards. The Gas House Gang were world champions.

Unlike the '27 Yanks and '76 Big Red Machine, the Gas House Gang was not a dynasty. They did not have good seasons in the two years preceding 1934 and then failed to win again until 1942, when it was a whole new team and no longer the Gas House boys. But for one magnificent year, they took the baseball world by storm.

It was also the high spot for the Deans. Paul Dean never again matched the skills of his rookie year, and soon faded from the majors. Dizzy had two more fine seasons, winning 28 and 24, until the All-Star Game injury in 1937. After that he lost the great fastball and also faded from baseball, though not from the scene. Ol' Diz later returned as a broadcaster and personality. You just couldn't keep a guy like Dizzy Dean down, just as you couldn't stop the Cards in 1934, the team known forever as the Gas House Gang.

Unlike the Gas House Gang, which rose to one magnificent, if improbable, season, Cincinnati's Redlegs have dominated the National League for more than half a decade beginning in 1970. The team was aptly nicknamed the Big Red Machine and has steamrollered over much of their opposition during that time.

Four times in seven years the Big Red Machine has gone to the World Series, and in two years, 1975 and 1976, they've come away winners. It's harder to reach the World Series in the '70s because of divisional play. There are two divisional winners in each league, and those two teams must meet in a three-of-five play-off to determine which goes to the Series.

The Big Red Machine, as the name might indicate, is primarily a hitting team. Just look at their 1976 lineup. Here are the eight starters with their batting average, homers, and RBIs. Pete Rose (.323, 10, 63), Joe Morgan (.320, 27, 111), Ken Griffey (.336, 6, 74), Johnny Bench (.234, 16, 74), Tony Perez (.260, 19, 91), George Foster (.306, 29, 121),

Cesar Geronimo (.307, 2, 49), and Dave Concepcion (.281, 9, 69).

These stats point out the great power and hitting ability of the Reds lineup, but they don't tell the whole story. For instance, Rose once again led the National League in hits with 215. Morgan stole 60 bases and won a Gold Glove in addition to everything else, and then was named the National League's Most Valuable Player for the second straight year. He is now often called the best all-around player in baseball.

Catcher Bench, despite an off-year, is one of the most feared sluggers in the game and its best defensive backstop. Perez, whose .265 average might not look like much, is one of baseball's best clutch hitters and a man who has driven in 90 or more runs for ten straight seasons. Leftfielder Foster emerged as a star and led the majors in runs batted in. Concepcion and Geronimo, like Morgan and Bench, are considered about the best fielders at their positions, short and centerfield.

The only apparent weakness in the club might be its pitching. The starters are suspect, but the bullpen is superb. Manager Sparky Anderson never hesitates in coming out to the mound and giving the hook to a hurler.

How did the Reds build themselves into a powerhouse and stay there for so long? After all, they didn't buy superstars, and the team was built before the free-agent era when players could jump around to where the price was right.

Looking backward, it can be seen that the Redlegs had built a very powerful team in the late 1950s. Even then they were hitters, with the likes of Ted Kluszewski, Gus Bell, Wally Post, and a youngster named Frank Robinson. The team never won a pennant, but by 1961 they had. That's when Robinson had become a superstar and was joined by Vada Pinson, Gordy Coleman, Leo Cardenas, and Don Blasingame, as well as some holdovers from the '50s. That club lost to the Yanks in the World Series and failed to repeat in the next few seasons. The personnel began changing.

Perhaps the beginning of the new era and the eventual Big Red Machine came in 1963, when a young second baseman named Pete Rose joined the Reds. Rose was a throwback to the old days of the game in that he never knew the meaning of quit and wasn't really satisfied with himself unless his uniform was dirty. It didn't take long for him to get the nickname of Charley Hustle.

It wasn't easy for a rookie to break in then, just as it hadn't been in the old days. Rose remembers how some of the vets resented him because it looked as if he was going to displace veteran Don Blasingame at second.

"I guess you could say the Reds were a cliquey team when I came up," he says. "I hate to break it down like this, but the white guys on the team wouldn't have anything to do with me. Anyway, I hung around with the black guys, and I have to give a lot of credit for my early success to Frank Robinson and Vada Pinson, the two stars of the team. Both of them were very generous with their time and helped me immensely. They were never too busy to teach me some of the things a big leaguer has to know. And they certainly didn't object to my hanging around with them."

Rose became a starter and hasn't been out of there since. Though not a slugger, Rose has become a great ball player, a three-time batting champion and lifetime .300 hitter who will soon join a very select club, those ball players with more than 3,000 lifetime hits. In an era when only the elite few

1976 Reds, "The Big Red Machine". Back Row, left to right: Bob Bailey, Dave Concepcion, Gary Nolan, Bill Plummer, Pat Zachry, Santo Alcala, Jack Billingham, Rawly Eastwick, Cesar Geronimo, Pedro Borbon, Mike Lum. Middle Row: Bernie Stowe, equipment manager; Paul Campbell, traveling secretary; Joel Youngblood, Don Gullett, Ed Armbrister, George Foster, Tony Perez, Johnny Bench, Ken Griffey, Will McEnaney, Dan Driessen, Mark Stowe, bat boy; Larry Starr, trainer. Front Row: Pete Rose, Joe Morgan, Russ Nixon, coach; Ted Kluszewski, coach; Larry Shepard, coach; Sparky Anderson, manager; George Scherger, coach; Fred Norman, Doug Flynn, Manny Sarmiento

had $100,000 contracts, Pete Rose announced that he was going to become "the first $100,000 singles hitter"—and he was.

A hustling, unselfish ball player, Rose has played second, third, and the outfield during his Cincinnati career, going wherever he can best help the team. His attitude has also rubbed off on his teammates.

"I might not have the talent of a Cesar Cedeno or Bobby Bonds," Pete once said. "Maybe I'm just a little bit above average. But I have more than average pride. That's why I'll always hustle and never change my style. I find the most difficult thing about being a big league ball player is maintaining the status you worked so hard to achieve.

"If you become known as a .300 hitter, a 20-game winner, or a 40-homer man, people expect you to stay at that level, and there are always those waiting for you to falter. . . .

". . . that's where the pride comes in. It drives you to keep your performance at a high level. I'm never going to give anyone a chance to say that Pete Rose doesn't put out anymore, or Pete Rose doesn't have what it takes; he's just hanging on. I'll know when it's time to quit, and I'll be the first to go."

So far that hasn't happened. Pete leads on. In the 1972 World Series when the Reds were trailing the Oakland A's, three games to one, Pete approached manager Anderson and said,

"Skip, you can give it to me out loud if you want. I've been lousy, and maybe the others will get the message."

Anderson had his chance when some reporters and other members of the team gathered around. When someone asked him about Pete's play, the manager simply said:

"Pete Rose is Cincinnati. He is the Reds."

But he wasn't the only one. Toward the late '60s the club added two more young sluggers, Tony Perez and Lee May, and then in 1968 they brought up twenty-year-old Johnny Bench to do the catching. Right then and there the Reds became contenders. Perez, May, and Bench gave the team power once again, while Rose, new second baseman Tommy Helms, and centerfielder Bobby Tolan added speed to the attack. As usual, the pitching was adequate, no better.

Yet by 1970 the team had won a pennant. Bench was the big gun with an MVP season, 45 home runs and 148 runs batted in. But the entire team contributed to the win. In the World Series, it was the Redlegs batters against the pitching-rich Baltimore Orioles.

The first two games were close, but Baltimore won each, 4-3 and 6-5. Then a 9-3 Oriole win seemed to put a lock on it. Cincy held on to win the fourth game, but the Orioles went on to wrap it in five.

The Reds tried again in 1972. The team made a big trade that year, sending second baseman Helms and first sacker May to Houston for Joe Morgan. Morgan was a pepperpot, standing just 5-9, but he brought an awful lot of talent to Cincy. He was a great glove man, ran extremely well, and hit for average and with power. As Rose said after playing with Morgan for a while,

"Joe is a great ball player. He's a winner and a hustler. Keep your eye on him when he's on the bases. He steals as well as anyone, but he never goes when we have a big lead, only when it means something for the team. He's not a glory boy and that's another reason why he's great."

With Morgan in the lineup, the Reds took their division, then whipped Pittsburgh in the play-offs to go into the

World Series. But once again they ran into a hot team. The Oakland A's won the first two games by 3-2 and 2-1 scores. Then Cincy took the third, 1-0, but Oakland won the fourth, 3-2. Cincy finally came to life to win the fifth and sixth games, 5-4 and 8-1. But Oakland won the seventh and deciding game, another one-run victory, 3-2.

It was a bitter loss for the Big Red Machine. They had come close again, and still not won the big one. The next year they suffered another disappointment when they lost to the New York Mets in the league play-offs. In 1974 the L.A. Dodgers won the Western Division.

The Big Red Machine had been a top team since 1970, but had not won a World Series. People were beginning to call them a choke team, a club that couldn't win the big one. In 1975 the club once again went out to try to prove themselves true champions.

This time it all jelled. The Redlegs took their division, won in the play-offs, and in seven hard-fought games whipped the Boston Red Sox in the World Series. They were finally champions. Now they had to prove it was no fluke. They wanted very much to win again in 1976.

With new young players like Foster, Geronimo, and Griffey in the lineup, the Big Red Machine seemed more powerful than ever. The club hit .280 for the year and ran away with the National League West. In the play-offs, the Redlegs then whipped a strong Philadelphia team in three straight games. It was back to the World Series for the fourth time in seven years. This time the opponent would be the New York Yankees, who were coming into their first fall classic since 1964.

The Redlegs wasted no time. In the first inning of the

opening game Morgan blasted a home run to give his team the lead. When it was over the Reds had ten hits and a 5-1 victory. They were off and running.

In the second game the Reds had to contend with Yankee ace Catfish Hunter. It was a close game all the way. It was tied at 3-3 when the Redlegs came to bat in the ninth. With two out, the Yankee shortstop made a throwing error on speedy Ken Griffey, who took second. An intentional walk to Morgan brought up Tony Perez, Mr. Clutch, who promptly singled home the winning run.

Then in the third game Cincy picked up three runs in the second and played that to a 6-2 victory. Now the Big Red Machine was a game away from a sweep. Sure enough, they closed it out with little trouble to take their second straight world championship.

Now everyone was calling the Big Red Machine the best in baseball, and there were comparisons made with the great teams of the past. Manager Anderson, the team's biggest booster, compared his club with the Brooklyn Dodgers of the late 1950s, the Dodgers of Robinson, Reese, Campanella, Hodges, Snider, and Furillo. The Redlegs came out on top at almost every position, according to Anderson. He also alluded to his club being on a par with the '27 Yankees.

It's difficult to compare old and recent teams since the game and players change. The '27 Yanks finally fell victim to the advancing age of some players and the rising Philadelphia A's. The '34 Cards had one magnificent season which they couldn't duplicate. The Reds also have seen some changes.

After the 1976 season the club's best pitcher, Don Gullett, played out his option and signed with the Yankees. The team then opted for young Dan Dreissen as the new first baseman and traded veteran clutch hitting Tony Perez to Montreal. Then came the money problems.

With the new free-agent system, ball players can play out their options and be free to negotiate with any team. The Reds, perhaps the closest team in baseball besides the best, suddenly found their payroll going sky high. Before the 1977 season began, a group of players were holding out, the most notable being Morgan and Rose.

Morgan claimed he keeps being told that he's the best in baseball and wants to be paid for it. He finally signed a three-year pact for about a million dollars. Then Rose bristled. The spirit of the Reds threatened to play out his option. He took some pot shots at everyone.

"Some of the younger players are trying to get too much too soon," he said. "I've been here fourteen years and was only the third highest-paid player last year. I'm trying to figure out why that is."

One by one the players signed. Rose was the last. He waited until just before the season began and wasn't completely satisfied at that. The Perez trade also angered some of the players who appreciated the contributions made on and off the field by the affable Tony. They doubted if Dreissen could produce as much.

So once where there was nothing but harmony, a team with a common goal, there is now much bitterness, with money being the prime concern. As of early 1977, the free agents in baseball were making big, big money on long-term contracts. It's hard to fault a player who knows he is good, when he wants to make hay while he can. Management has never shown loyalty to players. When the string is out, the player goes. Why should the players be expected to be loyal, to play for $75,000 out of loyalty, when they might get $200,000 somewhere else as a free agent?

The money game has changed baseball, and the modern game of baseball has a style of its own. Players on Murderers' Row or the Gas House Gang didn't worry about money. It was a purer game then; baseball the *game* was the important thing.

The Cincinnati Reds, the Big Red Machine, is surely one of baseball's superteams. Yet it may not be age or an eroding of skills that ends their reign—it may just be the modern game of baseball.

CHAPTER 7

The One and Only Jackie

His name was Jack Roosevelt Robinson. He played in the major leagues for only ten years. Yet he is in baseball's Hall of Fame. He didn't set a host of hitting or fielding records. Yet his achievements are as worthy as anyone's in baseball. The beginning of the 1977 season marked the thirtieth anniversary of Jackie Robinson's rookie season with the old Brooklyn Dodgers. It is an important date to remember.

Jackie Robinson was a player who *must* be remembered. He was the first black man to play baseball in the major leagues, and his experience in baseball was like no man's before or since.

Jackie Robinson was a great player. He was an outstanding hitter and fielder, a spark plug who could ignite an entire team with his dash and daring on the basepaths. His career was relatively short, but not because of an injury or illness. It was ended because Jackie was thirty-seven years old and slowing down. There were younger players ready to take his place.

It's possible that Jackie was ready for the majors ten years earlier. But since blacks didn't play before 1947, he was twenty-eight when he came to the Dodgers. It's hard to believe now that blacks have only been in the majors for some thirty years. But Jackie was the one who did it. Because of him, the likes of Willie Mays, Hank Aaron, Roberto Clemente, Frank Robinson, Bob Gibson, Reggie Jackson, and Joe Morgan were all able to follow. These men and many others and the entire sports world owe a debt to Jackie Robinson and his memory.

Jackie was born on January 31, 1919, in Cairo, Georgia. He was the last of five children born to Mallie and Jerry Robinson. Soon after Jackie was born his father left, being unable to handle the pressure put on poor black farmers during those days in Georgia. Mrs. Robinson was told to take her family from the farm where they had worked.

Not knowing where to go with five children, she finally spoke to one of her brothers who told her about life in California. In May 1920 she took her family to the West Coast, where they settled into a small apartment. Then Mrs. Robinson had to go to work to feed and clothe her family. That wasn't easy.

Little Jackie was almost like a mascot to the older children. He followed them around all day. When he was the only one too young for school, he went with them anyway, played in the sandbox all day, and then followed them home again in the afternoon. When the weather was bad, the teacher took him into the classroom.

Jackie's first baseball was made from old woolen socks, which were unraveled, then wound into a ball. Jackie would take a stick and hit the old ball for hours on end. When he finally went to school himself, his athletic ability soon made him popular. In fact, he didn't have to bring his own lunch because the other boys bribed him with food to get him on their team.

The fun and games didn't last long, however. Jackie had to join his brother and sisters in taking odd jobs to help bring a few more dollars into the family kitty. These jobs began to teach him what the white man's world was all about. He began to hear the slurs of racial prejudice hurled in his direction. Soon he was more aware of it, and he noticed it came from everywhere.

"I remember sweeping the sidewalk in front of our house," he said, "and a little girl came by and began yelling at me, 'Nigger, nigger, nigger.' "

When he got older, Jackie began getting into some trouble on the streets. He even made a quick trip to jail, but it was only for swimming illegally in a city reservoir. Fortunately, Jackie got some help before the trouble became worse. One man who helped him was a mechanic named Carl Anderson who had a shop near Jackie's house.

"Carl told me it took more guts to be different and say no to the gang," Jackie said. "And when I thought about the things he said they really got to me."

Soon sports began playing a larger part in Jackie's life. He played often at his church, where they had organized programs, and found he enjoyed baseball and football a lot more than hanging out on street corners. By the time Jackie reached Muir Technical High School he was already a top athlete, fast and strong.

"I enjoyed the competition and was always very aggressive," Jackie said. "I wanted to win and enjoyed the reputation of being the man to beat. But I also always placed an importance on being a team man and not a hotdog."

During the time he starred in high school Jackie began thinking about the future. He wanted to stay in sports and continue his education. That was a problem. There were a few blacks at the major colleges then, but not nearly as many as today. Colleges didn't want someone who'd speak out against things he didn't feel were right, and Jackie always spoke out. Without much of a choice, he enrolled at Pasadena Junior College, in California.

Jackie starred in football, basketball, baseball, and track. Once when a big track meet and baseball game were set for the same day, Jackie arranged to take his broad jumps in the morning. He went out there alone with just the officials and leaped 25 feet, 6½ inches, setting a new record for a junior college athlete. Then he rushed back to play the baseball game. He was a .417 hitter that year, with 25 stolen bases in 24 games.

It was 1938 then, and one afternoon a veteran baseball star, Jimmie Dykes, saw Jackie play for Pasadena. After the game he walked up to Jackie's coach and said:

"That Robinson kid could play major league baseball at a moment's notice."

Jackie spoke out, even then. He was the only black starter on the Pasadena basketball team. The white players didn't bother him because he was a star, but really gave it to the other blacks, the subs. Finally, Jackie rebelled, saying he wouldn't play in any more games unless the whites cooled it. They did.

After finishing at Pasadena, Jackie got a scholarship to UCLA, where he became an immediate football sensation as a halfback. In fact, he was so good in a game against Stanford that the Stanford coach said,

"Jackie Robinson is the greatest backfield runner I've seen in all my connection with football. I've seen a lot of grid greats, like Ernie Nevers and Eddie Mahan, and other great broken field runners, but this kid Robinson can do it better than all of them."

Jackie was good, all right. He led the nation in rushing with an average of more than twelve yards a carry, a fantastic mark. From there, Jackie went on to star in basketball and baseball. As an athlete he could do it all, yet he still didn't know what the future held. He had already met Rachel Isum, who would later become his wife, and in some ways he was a confused young man.

"I decided to leave ULCA after two years," he said, "because I became convinced that no amount of education would help a black man get a job. I felt I was living in an academic and athletic dream world. It was time for me to help my mother and my family."

It was 1941 now and Jackie found a job as an assistant athletic director at a work camp sponsored by the National Youth Administration. He was helping poor youngsters to stay off the streets and learn about sports, much as he had done. But the job didn't last long. In December 1941 the Japanese bombed Pearl Harbor and the United States entered World War II.

Jackie entered the army. Once again he bumped head-on into the white man's world. He had to fight to get into Officer's Candidate School, then he fought to rid the base of segregation.

Things came to a head when Jackie refused to move to the back of an army bus, which was being driven by a civilian. An argument started and soon a military policeman took the side of the driver. The army brought court-martial charges against Jackie. But he fought them and won. By then the war was ending and Jackie applied for and received a discharge.

Jackie took a coaching job at Sam Houston College, a small black school in Texas. He didn't stay there long. Soon afterward he joined the Kansas City Monarchs, one of the top baseball teams in the old Negro Leagues.

The Monarchs paid Jackie $400 a month to play for the Monarchs. Life in the Negro Leagues wasn't easy. There were long, tiring bus rides to distant locations. Once there, the accommodations were poor and the food even worse. Even when the competition was first-rate, the game might be ruined by a terrible playing field. There was always the threat of running into racial prejudice.

But the black teams and black players endured. There were many great players in the Negro Leagues, players who would have been equally great in the majors but never had the chance. Players like Josh Gibson, Satchel Paige, and others made black history and are just now getting the true recognition they deserve.

It was early 1945 now, and what Jackie didn't know was that a man named Branch Rickey was scouting the Negro Leagues for players. Rickey ran the Brooklyn Dodgers and was a wily baseball man who had a new and daring plan in mind. He covered it up by saying he was thinking of starting a new Negro League which would have only top players. That's why he was scouting so much.

What Rickey really wanted to do was to bring black players to the major leagues. Some people were beginning to call for it, but Rickey kept his plan a secret.

"I didn't tell anyone," he said; "no one in the world what I really had in mind. I had spent some $35,000 scouting Negro players, but the baseball people were the last ones I wanted to know about it."

At the same time, Jackie and two other blacks went up to Boston because they heard the Red Sox were going to give blacks a tryout. The three got the runaround for about four days, then were given a short tryout. Jackie could tell it wasn't the real thing, but the pressure was growing.

Rickey heard about the tryout and asked black sports-writer Wendell Smith if any of the black players were good enough for the majors.

"Yeah," answered Smith, quickly. "Jackie Robinson's good enough. He could play in any league."

Rickey knew he would need one special kind of man to be the first black. He began having scouts look at Jackie. The more he learned, the more interested he became. He had also looked at such future Dodger stars as Don Newcombe and Roy Campanella, but didn't feel they were quite right to be the first.

Jackie's clean life style was just right for Rickey. The only negative thing went something like this: "Robinson is a smart guy whose major fault is that he likes to argue with white people."

Rickey finally exploded: "From what I can see, Robinson's biggest crime so far was being born a Negro. If he had done the things people are criticizing him for as a white player he would have been praised to the skies as a fighter, a holler guy, a real competitor, a ball player's ball player. But because he's black, his aggressiveness is offensive to some white people. That doesn't change my opinion of him. From what I've learned, I think he's the man I want. Now I'd like to meet him and talk with him."

The two met for the first time on August 28, 1945. Jackie

still didn't know why he was there. He thought Rickey wanted to start a new Negro League, so that's what Jackie began talking about.

"No," interrupted Rickey. "That's not the reason, Jackie. You were brought here to play for the Brooklyn organization, perhaps, as a start, for Montreal."

Jackie's mouth dropped in disbelief. Before he could say anything, the older man began explaining his plan.

"Jackie, we've got no army," said Rickey. "There's virtually no one on our side. No owners, no umpires, very few newspapermen. And I'm afraid that many fans will be hostile. We'll be in a tough spot. We can win only if we can convince them that I'm doing this because you're a great ball player, a fine gentleman."

Immediately Jackie felt a surge of pressure come down on his shoulders like a lead weight. That pressure and stress would stay with him for almost his entire career. He also saw the great possibilities in what Branch Rickey was saying. If he was the one to do it, so be it. He couldn't walk away.

Rickey then went about telling Jackie what he could expect and how he'd have to react. Rickey's directness almost shocked Jackie in what is now remembered as a milestone confrontation in sports.

"Suppose I'm an opposing player rounding first in a crucial game," Rickey snapped. "I charge into second and we have a close play. We collide. I lunge toward you and I shout, 'Get out of the way, you dirty black son of a bitch!' What do you do?"

Jackie started to say something, but Rickey shouted him down . . . "You're playing shortstop and I come down from first, stealing, flying in spikes high. I cut you in the leg. Then

I grin at you and say, 'Now how do you like that, nigger boy?' What do you do?"

Now Jackie was fuming, but Rickey continued, giving him more examples of game situations. Jackie broke out in a cold sweat. He thought about all the years of fighting prejudice that had already gone before him. Finally, he spoke.

"Mr. Rickey," he said, "do you want a ball player who's afraid to fight back?"

Rickey answered without pausing.

"I want a ball player with guts enough not to fight back!"

Then he continued. "Jackie, this is one battle we can't fight our way through . . . because there's no one with us, no one to back us up. This is a battle in which you'll have to swallow an awful lot of pride and count on base hits and stolen bases to do the job."

When it all ended, Rickey offered Jackie a bonus of $3,500 and a salary of $600 a month to play for the Montreal Royals, the Dodgers' top farm team which had also never had a black player before. Jackie accepted and the two men shook hands. Then Rickey said:

"Jackie, I just want to beg two things of you. First, that as a ball player you give it your utmost. And, secondly, as a man you give continuing fidelity to your race and to this crucial cause that you symbolize."

The news caused a furor in the baseball world. Everyone had an opinion, with most people opposed to Jackie's playing. Some just didn't want blacks, period. Others thought the time wasn't right. Still others figured he just wasn't good enough, especially with so many ball players returning from the army for the 1946 season.

Jackie and Rachel were married before the season and traveled to Florida together for spring training. They ran into prejudice right from the start and had a terrible time just making travel connections and then finding places to eat. Locating living quarters was equally hard. They finally had to stay with black families in town, people who were usually poor to begin with and living in bad conditions.

There was another black on the Montreal roster that year, a pitcher named John Wright, who never really made it. But the two started together. The manager at Montreal was Clay Hopper. He was from Mississippi and had many prejudices against blacks. In fact, during spring training Jackie made a great stop at second and Rickey said to Hopper,

"No other human could have made that play."

Hopper answered:

"Mr. Rickey, do you really think he's human?"

By the end of that year Clay Hopper was to tell Branch Rickey that Jackie was not only a great ball player, but a gentleman as well.

Yet there was a long way to go. Jackie worried about many things to begin with, not the least of which was just making the team.

"I understood that my being on that field was a symbol of the Negro's emerging self-respect," he said, "of a deep belief that somehow we had begun a magnificent era of Negro progress, a period in which Negroes could walk onto a baseball field, or into another area of life, asking no quarter, no special concessions, and compete creditably with white men. I went to practice determined to show manager Hopper that I could really play baseball."

By the time the Montreal team headed north, Jackie had won the second base job. Jackie will never forget his first game against the Jersey City Giants. His nervousness left by the third inning, partially because he hit a long home run into the left-field seats.

"I was so excited, so exhilarated, as I circled those bases that it seemed all the oxygen had left my brain and for a moment those stands were just a blur in front of me. As I crossed home plate two teammates were waiting to shake hands."

It wasn't all easy. Road games were the hardest, when many fans and players taunted Jackie. But Montreal got a big lead and Jackie was leading the league in hitting. That helped. When others tried to get him, Jackie remembered what Branch Rickey had said and swallowed his pride, answering with more base hits and great play. Near the end of the year one sportswriter was talking about the seasons of some of the major league stars, then added:

". . . but the greatest performance being put on anywhere in sport . . . is being supplied by . . . Jackie Robinson of Montreal who is playing baseball under pressures that would have crushed a less courageous man."

Others also praised Jackie's efforts. Bruno Betzel, manager of the rival Jersey City team, said, "I would like to have nine Jackie Robinsons playing on my team. If I had only one . . . I would room with him myself and put him to bed nights to make sure nothing happened to him."

When the season ended Jackie's stats bore out the praise. He led the league with a .349 average in 124 games, hit only three homers, but drove in 66 runs. He scored 113 times and was second in stolen bases. Now the question was where he'd be playing in 1947.

At first Jackie was listed on the Montreal roster. Branch Rickey was still carefully laying the groundwork. He took

Jackie Robinson (*Los Angeles Dodgers*)

the Dodgers to Cuba during spring training and let them play against some Cuban teams so they'd be used to playing on the same field with blacks. Then he contacted many prominent black leaders and asked them to try to keep black fans from making too much of a fuss over Jackie. No Jackie Robinson Days or Nights or anything like that. There'd be enough pressure as is.

The other problem was that Brooklyn had a good second baseman in Eddie Stanky. That was Jackie's position, but Rickey felt it best to try Jackie at first, where the Dodgers were still unsettled. Then Rickey talked to the young man once again.

"Jackie," he said, "last year is already ancient history. Now you've got to show these guys all over again. You've got to make the grade against major league pitching. I want you to concentrate on hitting the ball, getting on base any way you can. I want you to run wild, steal the pants off them, be the most prominent player on the field. Make everyone demand that you play with the Dodgers."

Some of the veteran Dodger players had drawn up a petition, trying to keep Jackie off the team, but Rickey quickly took care of that. At the end of spring training Montreal and the Dodgers played each other almost every day. After seven games Jackie was hitting .625 and had seven stolen bases. Then on April 10, 1947, Rickey passed out a press release.

"Brooklyn announces the purchase of the contract of Jack Roosevelt Robinson from Montreal. He will report immediately."

It had finally happened. After so many years of closed doors, a black man would be playing in the major leagues. Jackie Robinson would be the starting first baseman for the Brooklyn Dodgers.

Jackie started slowly. He was nervous and didn't get a hit in his first twenty times at bat. Most of his teammates were beginning to accept him. As one veteran said:

"Having Jackie on the team is a bit strange. It's like anything else new. We just don't know how to act with him, but I'm sure it will come in time. He'll be accepted. Other sports have had Negroes. Why not baseball? If he can win games, that's all I ask."

There were some problems, and none worse than with the Philadelphia Phillies, led by their manager, Alabama-born Ben Chapman. When the Dodgers came into Philly they really gave Jackie the business.

"Hey, nigger," someone yelled. "Why don't you go back to the cotton field where you belong!"

Another shouted: "Hey, snowflake, which one of those white boys' wives are you dating tonight?"

The players kept this up for several innings. Finally second baseman Stanky had had enough. He growled over to the Phillies dugout:

"Listen, you yellow-bellied cowards, why don't you yell at somebody who can answer back?"

Then shortstop Pee Wee Reese walked over and put his arm around Jackie's shoulder. It was a sign that the Dodgers were going to stick together, and that Jackie was one of them. Later Branch Rickey commented on how the Phillies really helped.

"They did more than anyone else to make the other Dodgers speak up in Jackie's behalf. When they abused Jackie like that they solidified and unified thirty men, for no one was willing to sit by and see someone kick around a man who had his hands tied behind his back."

Soon Jackie began to hit, and once he was getting on base,

he began stealing them. When he wasn't stealing he was driving pitchers crazy by threatening to go. On the field he was responding and playing great ball.

Off the field it was still tough. He and his family had to listen to every kind of racial slur imaginable. There were even threats against his and Rachel's life. There was a threatened protest strike by the St. Louis team which was put down by the National League president.

Jackie continued to play well through it all, and when the year ended, he had helped bring the Dodgers a National League pennant. He also finished with a .297 average in 150 games, including 175 hits, 31 doubles, five triples, 12 homers, and 48 RBIs. He also scored 125 times and led the league with 29 stolen bases. The *Sporting News* named him Rookie of the Year.

Unfortunately, the Dodgers were beaten in the World Series by the New York Yankees. Jackie hit .259 in the seven games. The big thing, of course, was that he played, something unheard of in previous years.

By 1948 several other teams began signing black players. They realized that there was no way to stop blacks from playing, and since the game was essentially a business, they had better start looking for the best players, white or black. Roy Campanella joined the Dodgers in 1948, followed by Don Newcombe. The Cleveland Indians signed Larry Doby in '48. Soon others followed. As hard as it may seem to believe now, only four years after Jackie broke the color line, a young player named Willie Mays signed with the Giants.

Despite getting through the first year, 1948 proved a tough one for Jackie. He had made many personal appearances in the off-season and was overweight when the new season started. Stanky had been traded to the Giants and

Jackie was now at second. Perhaps the pressure of the first year also caused a letdown. Jackie still did all right, with a .296 average, 12 homers, and 85 RBIs. But it wasn't what Rickey expected. Before the next season started he decided to do something else.

"I had to turn Jackie loose. I know insisting he turn the other cheek the first two years was right, but now it was time to let him be on his own. I told him so and saw that he welcomed my blessing. I knew he would now show the National League a thing or two."

It was a different Robinson in 1949. Early in the season one of his old tormentors from the Phillies began razzing him, not the old hateful stuff, but enough to get Jackie burning. He walked right up to the man and growled:

"Listen, you yellow SOB. I haven't forgotten those days in 1947 when you called me some unprintable filthy names, and I couldn't talk back. Well, I can talk back now, and I just want to tell you that if you say one more word to me or about me, I'll kick the hell out of you."

The man left quickly. Jackie had made his point, and he'd make it again many times before the season ended. He was also playing the best baseball of his life. At age thirty, he was at his playing peak. When the All-Star Game voting came around, Jackie got more than two million votes, the most in the league. He was the first black to play in an All-Star Game. And he kept the pace up the second half of the season. When it ended the Dodgers had another pennant and Jackie Robinson was the Most Valuable Player in the National League.

He deserved it all right. He led the league with a .342 batting average, getting 203 hits. He belted 16 homers and drove in 124 runs. He also led the league in stolen bases with

37. The only thing that put a damper on the season was another World Series loss to the Yanks.

Jackie settled into a good playing groove the next years. His averages read .328, .338, .308, .329, and .311. He showed he was a bona fide .300 hitter. The racial stuff also died down as new black players began coming into the league. What had been a unique event was now becoming commonplace.

During these years Jackie often spoke up off the field, and once again had the reputation of a troublemaker. He appeared on a television show in 1953 and charged that the New York Yankees, one of the last teams without blacks, with discrimination. The whole thing drew a lot of publicity and Jackie's enemies list grew. There was also some trouble in the Dodger organization. Owner Walter O'Malley forced Branch Rickey to resign. Jackie didn't like this and never really got along with O'Malley.

But he kept playing well on the field. The Dodgers had a great team in the late 1940s and early '50s. Their names are household words to all fans: Snider, Hodges, Reese, Furillo, Cox, Gilliam, Roe, Labine, Newcombe, Black, Campanella, and Jackie Robinson. They won pennants again in 1952, 1953, and 1955. They just kept losing to the Yanks in the Series, until 1955, when Jackie was part of the team that brought the first and only championship to Brooklyn.

Jackie was as much of a bench jockey as anyone now and is often remembered for his heated exchanges with Leo Durocher, his first manager and then manager of the rival Giants.

"Jockeying wakes a club up," Jackie said. "Often I would go to the park and feel that the club was down, was dead, and needed some shaking up. I could usually do it by riding the other bench. Any kind of crazy thing would do. Once I accused Durocher of wearing his wife's perfume and got a lot of mileage out of that."

Jackie began losing some of his speed around 1953. The Dodgers moved him from second to third that year, and he also played some outfield. Weight was always a problem and he was having trouble with his feet. He hit .311 that year, but only in 124 games. In fact, he himself admitted that, "I seriously considered quitting after 1954. . . . But there was still too much baseball in my blood. I wanted to play."

It must have been hard for Jackie, knowing he lost all those years to discrimination. His career just wasn't that long and he didn't want to give it up. In the World Series year of 1955 he hit just .256 in 105 games. It looked as if the end was near. He hated to go out with a season like that.

"Baseball is like a poker game," he said. "Nobody wants to quit when he's losing; nobody wants you to quit when you're ahead."

He worked hard for 1956. It wasn't easy. He would be classed as a utility man that year, playing five different positions. Now and then he'd flash his old form, but he couldn't do it every day. As one writer put it:

"His joints seemed stiffer than ever, and getting off the bench every inning became more and more of an ordeal. Age had taken its toll, but the turn of events also robbed Robinson of the challenges that had fired him up in years past."

Playing part-time Jackie did well enough. He batted .275 in 117 games, getting 10 homers and driving in 43 runs. The Dodgers won another pennant that year and once again faced the Yanks in the World Series. Knowing Jackie was a great clutch player, the team started him at third in all seven games. He managed a .250 average with a homer and two ribbys. The Dodgers, of course, lost again.

Jackie was thinking about retirement all over again when he learned he had been traded to the Giants. That was one thing he couldn't do, not now—play for his hated rivals. He decided to call it quits.

It would be nice to say that life was good to Jackie after retirement, but, unfortunately, that wasn't true. There were ups and downs, but too many downs. Working was no problem. Jackie got a good job with a major corporation and was involved in many other business ventures. In 1962 he learned he had been elected to baseball's Hall of Fame. It was well-earned and richly deserved.

There was still plenty of controversy, though. Jackie still spoke up on matters of equal rights and discrimination. He had many friends and his share of enemies. Though he and his family lived in a large home in the suburbs, his oldest son, Jackie, Jr., began to get in trouble with the law. Later he became involved in drugs. He finally licked the problem and was on the road back when he was tragically killed in an auto accident in 1971.

During this time Jackie's own health began failing. Perhaps it was all those years of pressure-filled living, all that stress and anxiety, plus the wear and tear on his body. He contracted diabetes, then suffered a heart attack. He was only fifty years old at the time.

Jackie listened to the doctors, lost a great deal of weight, and slowed down his hectic work schedule. Yet he still continued to exist in the public light, speaking out whenever he felt it needed to be done. One of the things he wanted to see most was a black manager in baseball. Despite blacks being in the game for twenty-five years, there had never been a black manager.

He wasn't to see this happen. On October 24, 1972, Jackie

Robinson died suddenly of a second heart attack. He was just fifty-three years old.

Tributes to Jackie poured in from all over the country. All of them were sincere, for whether people liked him or not, most had to admire and respect this courageous man and great ball player, who perhaps started a major sports career under more pressure than any man in history.

In the fall of 1974, one of Jackie's strongest wishes finally came true. It was announced that the great outfielder, Frank Robinson, no relation to Jackie, was being named the first black manager in baseball history. He would pilot the Cleveland Indians in 1975. At a large press conference, Frank Robinson spoke to reporters and newsmen. He talked mainly about what he would do as a manager and the kind of team he expected the Indians to be. Then he suddenly looked solemn.

"If I had one wish in the world today," he said quietly, "it would be that Jackie Robinson could be here to see this happen."

There were very few people listening who wouldn't have wanted the same thing.

Index

Aaron, Hank, 45, 90–91, 108, 111, 109–115, 170
Alexander, Grover Cleveland, 15, 144
Altrock, Nick, 122
American League, 17, 21, 22, 29, 67, 122, 145, 148
Anderson, Carl, 171
Anderson, Sparky, 160, 163, 166
Anderson, Wayne, 126
Appalachian League, 134

Bacharach Giants, 30
Baltimore Elite Giants, 30
Baltimore Orioles, 64, 93, 164
Banks, Ernie, 90, 133
Base stealing, 8, 67–80
Bell, Gus, 160
Bench, Johnny, 12, 34–38, 143, 159, 160, 164
Berra, Yogi (Lawrence Peter), 11, 26–29, 33, 36, 40, 103
Billingham, Jack, 114
Binghamton, 4
Black, Joe, 33
Blanchard, John, 103
Blasingame, Don, 161
Boston Braves, 42, 198. *See also* Braves
Boston Red Sox, 12, 54, 57, 72, 93, 106–107
Braves, 110, 112, 114–115
Bresnahan, Roger, 10
Brett, George, 46
Brock, Lou, 8, 68–69, 80–88
Brown, Mace, 17
Brye, Steve, 137
Bunting, 49, 64

California Angels, 135
Campanella, Roy, 11, 29–33, 175, 183
Cantillon, Joe, 120
Cardenas, Leo, 161
Carew, Rod, 7, 8, 45–46, 59–66, 68
Carl, King, 16
Carleton, Tex, 151
Cashman, Joe, 17
Catchers, 7–8, 9–43
Cedeno, Cesar, 46, 68
Chapman, Ben, 182
Chase, Hal, 74
Chicago Cubs, 13, 16, 21, 74, 81, 82
Cincinnati Reds, 8, 12, 34, 42–43, 114, 141, 142, 155, 159–168
Clemente, Roberto, 45, 109, 170
Cleveland Indians, 103
Cobb, Ty (Tyrus Raymond), 7, 8, 10, 44, 45, 47–50, 55, 63, 65, 69–76, 77, 79, 84, 86, 88, 118–119, 122
Cochrane, Mickey (Frank King), 11, 17–22, 156
Coleman, Gordy, 161
Collins, Rip, 10, 151–155
Combs, Earle, 25, 142, 144, 145, 147, 148
Concepcion, Dave, 143, 160
Cox, Billy, 31
Crawford, Sam, 122
Criger, Lou, 72, 73
Cronin, Joe, 16, 58

Davis, Spud, 156
Dean, Daffy (Paul), 142, 152, 153, 155, 156, 159
Dean, Dizzy (Jay Hanna), 142, 151–153, 155, 156, 157, 158, 159
DeLancy, Bell, 151
Detroit Tigers, 21, 70, 72, 137, 156–158
Dickey, Bill, 11, 17, 22–26, 40
DiMaggio, Joe, 25, 45, 81, 102, 109
Dobson, Joe, 57
Doby, Larry, 183
Dodgers, 11, 29, 31, 76, 110, 126, 128, 169
Dover, 20
Downing, Al, 115
Dreisser, Dan, 166
Drysdale, Don, 126
Dugan, Joe, 142, 143
Dunn, Jack, 93
Durocher, Leo, 142, 151, 185, 186
Dykes, Jimmie, 172

Eastern Shore League, 20
Elberfeld, Kid, 70, 72
Emery balls, 47
Evans, Billy, 145
Evers, Johnny, 74

Fastballs, 117–119, 135, 137, 140, 144, 152
Feller, Bob, 100, 116
Fisher, Jack, 106
Fisk, Carlton, 12, 42
Flamethrowers, 8, 116–140
Foley, Jimmy, 25–26

Foster, George, 143, 159, 160, 165
Fowler, Dick, 58
Foxx, Jimmy, 16, 98, 100
Frick, Ford, 106
Frisch, Frankie, 142, 151, 153, 155, 156, 157
Furillo, Carl, 31

Garagiola, Joe, 27
Gehrig, Lou, 16, 25, 96, 143, 145, 147, 148, 150
Gehringer, Charlie, 156
Geraghty, Ben, 110
Geronomo, Cesar, 143, 160, 165
Giants, 13, 16, 124, 143, 155, 183
Gibson, Bob, 130, 170
Gibson, Josh, 174
Giliam, Jim, 33
Golden Glove Award, 37, 160
Greenberg, Hank, 100, 156, 158
Griffey, Ken, 143, 159, 165, 166
Grimm, Charley, 16
Grove, Lefty, 116
Gullett, Don, 166

Hadley, Bump, 21, 22
Hall of Fame, 11, 15, 44, 135, 142, 152, 187
Hartnett, Gabby, 11, 13–18
Hayes, Frank, 58
Heilmann, Harry, 44, 54
Helms, Tommy, 164
Hodges, Gil, 31
Holtzman, Ken, 61
Home run hitters, 8, 89–115
Hopper, Clay, 178
Hornsby, Roger, 44, 45, 47, 51–53, 144, 149, 151
Howard, Elston, 40, 103
Howard, Frank, 126
Hoyt, Waite, 123, 142, 143, 145, 149
Hubbell, Carl, 16, 158
Huggins, Miller, 142
Hundley, Randy, 37
Hunter, Catfish, 166
Huston, Til, 143

Indianapolis Clowns, 110
International League, 41

Jackson, Joe, 44, 45
Jackson, Reggie, 170
Jacksonville, 110
Johnson, Walter, 7, 8, 10, 50, 116–128, 139, 140

Kansas City Monarchs, 174
Kansas City Royals, 103, 137
Killebrew, Harmon, 90
Kluszewski, Ted, 126, 160
Koenig, Mark, 142, 144, 149
Koufax, Sandy, 7, 8, 116, 117, 125–134, 135, 138, 139
Kubek, Tony, 103

Labine, Clem, 33
Lajoie, Napoleon, 10, 44, 45
Landis, Kenesaw Mountain, 158
Lazzeri, Tony, 142, 144, 145, 147, 148, 149
Larsen, Don, 29
Little Rock, 25
Lopes, Davey, 68
Lopez, Hector, 103

McBride, Bake, 87
McCarthy, Joe, 17, 57
McGraw, John, 13
Mack, Connie, 21, 145
Madlock, Bill, 46
Maloney, Jim, 36
Mantle, Mickey, 26, 45, 90, 102, 103, 105, 106, 109, 113
Maris, Roger, 90, 102–107, 113
Martin, Pepper, 21, 142, 151, 156, 157
Mathews, Eddie, 90, 113
May, Lee, 164
Mays, Willie, 45, 90, 109, 183
Medwick, Joe "Ducky," 142, 151, 158
Meusel, Bob, 25, 142, 143, 145, 147, 149
Minnesota Twins, 45, 57, 60, 61, 137
Montreal Royals, 1, 176, 178
Moore, Wilcy, 149
Morgan, Joe, 68, 143, 159, 160, 164, 166, 167
Most Valuable Player Award, 11, 12, 19, 29, 31, 33, 37, 42, 103, 130, 142, 143, 148, 160, 164, 184
Mullin, Willard, 153, 155
Munson, Thurmon, 12, 34, 38–43
Musial, Stan, 45, 81

Nashua, 31
National League, 37, 41, 45, 54, 67, 142, 159
Negro National League, 30–31
Newcombe, Don, 29, 31, 33, 81, 175, 183
New England League, 31

Newsom, Bobo, 100
New York Mets, 29, 129, 134
New York Yankees, 8, 11, 12, 18, 21, 22, 25, 28, 38, 40, 42–43, 65, 95, 105, 106, 141, 142–150, 161, 183, 185
Norfolk, 27

Oakland A's, 163, 164
Osteen, Claude, 139–140
Otis, Amos, 68
Owen, Marv, 158

Pacific Coast League, 20
Paige, Satchel, 174
Pennock, 142, 143, 145, 148, 149
Perez, Tony, 143, 159, 164, 167
Perkins, Cy, 20
Philadelphia Athletics, 18, 21, 87, 144
Philadelphia Phillies, 182
Piedmont League, 28
Pinson, Vada, 161
Pipgras, George, 142, 149
Pittsburgh Pirates, 17, 124, 149
Portland, 20
Post, Wally, 160

Reese, Pee Wee, 31
Richardson, Bobby, 103
Rickey, Branch, 31, 174, 175, 176, 178, 179, 181, 185
Rivers, Mickey, 68
Rizzuto, Phil, 25, 33
Robinson, Frank, 61, 90, 160–161, 170, 188
Robinson, Jackie, 8, 31, 45, 81, 111, 169–188
Roe, Preacher, 33
Rookie of the Year, 37, 41, 61
Root, Charley, 16, 17
Rose, Pete, 45, 46, 70, 115, 143, 154, 159, 160, 161–162
Rowe, Schoolboy, 156, 157
Ruppert, Jacob, 143
Ruth, Babe (George Herman), 7, 8, 16, 25, 53–54, 89–93, 95, 98, 102, 113, 142, 143, 144, 145, 147, 148, 149, 150
Ryan, Nolan, 8, 116, 117, 134–140

Saint Louis Browns, 26
Saint Louis Cardinals, 8, 12, 21, 22, 68, 82, 107, 141, 142, 144, 150–159
San Diego Padres, 88
Schalk, Ray, 10
Seaver, Tom, 116
Shawkey, Bob, 143
Sherry, Norm, 129
Shocker, Urban, 149
Simmons, Al, 16
Simmons, Ted, 12
Sisler, George, 44, 45, 54
Skowron, Bill, 103
Smith, Wandell, 175
Snider, Duke, 31
Southern Associates, 25
Spitballs, 47, 49, 81
Stanky, Eddie, 181, 182, 183
Stein, Herb, 60
Street, Gabby, 10, 118, 125
Syracuse, 41

Tanana, Frank, 139
Terry, Bill, 44, 45, 54, 65
Thomson, Bobby, 112
Tinker, Joe, 74
Tolan, Bobby, 164

Veach, Bobby, 122
Vitt, Oscar, 50

Waddell, Rube, 116
Walsh, Ed, 49
Washington Senators, 117, 122, 143
Western League, 135
White, Bill, 42
Williams, Ted, 8, 44, 45, 54–59, 63, 65
Wills, Maury, 69, 76–81, 84, 85, 86, 88
Woodling, Gene, 40
World Series, 16 (1932); 17 (1938); 19; 21 (1931); 21 (1934); 22, 24 (1943); 25; 29 (1956); 31 (1947, 1949, 1952, 1955); 33 (1944); 42 (1976); 74 (1907); 84; 123–124 (1924); 125 (1925); 128 (1959); 130 (1963); 133; 149; 150 (1928, 1929, 1930, 1931, 1932); 156; 161; 163 (1972); 164 (1970); 164–165 (1972, 1975); 165–166 (1976); 185; 186
Wright, John, 178

Yastrzemski, Carl, 45
Young, Cy, 72, 73, 119; Award, 130, 133

Zachery, Tom, 148

ABOUT THE AUTHOR

Bill Gutman is a free-lance writer who has written both fiction and nonfiction, much of it in the sports field. He was born in New York City and grew up in Stamford, Connecticut. Mr. Gutman received a B.A. in English Literature from Washington College in Chestertown, Maryland, and has done graduate work at the University of Bridgeport.

He began his writing career as a reporter and feature writer for *Greenwich Time*, a daily newspaper in Greenwich, Connecticut. He later became the paper's Sports Editor. After a brief fling in the advertising field, he returned to writing full time.

Mr. Gutman has written books on all the major sports, including biographies of Pistol Pete Maravich, O. J. Simpson, and Hank Aaron. He's also written a biography of jazz great Duke Ellington. His fiction has appeared in Fawcett's baseball and football annuals, in *Boys' Life* magazine, and has been collected in a book published by Julian Messner. He presently makes his home in Wilton, Connecticut.